D0193254

To: _____

The LORD gathers the lambs in his arms and carries them close to his heart; he gently leads those that have young.

ISAIAH 40:11

From: _____

God's Words of Life for Moms
Copyright 2000 by The Zondervan Corporation

ISBN 0-310-98051-8

Excerpts taken from *The Mom's Devotional Bible; New International Version* with devotions written by Elisa Morgan. Copyright © 1996 by The Zondervan Corporation. All rights reserved.

All Scripture quotations, unless otherwise noted, are taken from the *Holy Bible: New International Version*®. Copyright © 1973, 1978, 1984, by International Bible Society. Used by permission of ZondervanPublishingHouse. All rights reserved.

The "NIV" and "New International Version" trademarks are registered in the United States Patent and Trademark Office by International Bible Society.

All devotions included in this book were written by Elisa Morgan, President and CEO of MOPS International, Inc.

Requests for information should be addressed to:
    Inspirio, the Gift Group of Zondervan
    Grand Rapids, Michigan 49530

Assistant editor: Molly C. Detweiler
Project editor: Sarah M. Hupp
Designer: David Carlson

Printed in China
00 01 02 03 /HK/ 4 3 2 1

GOD'S WORDS OF LIFE

for

Moms

from the
NEW INTERNATIONAL VERSION

BY

ELISA MORGAN

MOTHERS OF
MOPS.
PRESCHOOLERS

inspirio
The gift group of Zondervan

ANGER

Everyone should be quick to listen, slow to speak and slow to become angry, for man's anger does not bring about the righteous life that God desires.
JAMES 1:19–20

"In your anger do not sin": Do not let the sun go down while you are still angry.
EPHESIANS 4:26

Starting a quarrel is like breaching a dam;
    so drop the matter before a dispute breaks out.
PROVERBS 17:14

A gentle answer turns away wrath,
    but a harsh word stirs up anger.
PROVERBS 15:1

Do not be quickly provoked in your spirit,
    for anger resides in the lap of fools.
ECCLESIASTES 7:9

Better a patient man than a warrior,
    a man who controls his temper than one who
    takes a city.
PROVERBS 16:32

A patient man calms a quarrel.

PROVERBS 15:18

I want men everywhere to lift up holy hands in prayer, without anger or disputing.

1 TIMOTHY 2:8

Love is patient, love is kind. It does not envy, it does not boast, it is not proud. It is not rude, it is not self-seeking, it is not easily angered, it keeps no record of wrongs.

1 CORINTHIANS 13:4–5

The LORD is compassionate and gracious,
    slow to anger, abounding in love.
He will not always accuse,
    nor will he harbor his anger forever.

PSALM 103:8–9

Each one should test his own actions. Then he can take pride in himself, without comparing himself to somebody else.

GALATIANS 6:4

Be kind and compassionate to one another, forgiving each other, just as in Christ God forgave you. Be imitators of God, therefore, as dearly loved children and live

7

*a life of love, just as Christ loved us and gave himself up
for us as a fragrant offering and sacrifice to God.*
EPHESIANS 4:32—5:1-2

*Jesus said, "I tell you that anyone who is angry with his
brother will be subject to judgment. ... Therefore, if you
are offering your gift at the altar and there remember
that your brother has something against you, leave your
gift there in front of the altar. First go and be reconciled
to your brother; then come and offer your gift."*
MATTHEW 5:22-24

Who is a God like you,
> who pardons sin and forgives the transgression
> of the remnant of his inheritance?
You do not stay angry forever
> but delight to show mercy.
MICAH 7:18

DEVOTIONAL THOUGHT
ON ANGER

Is it possible to be good, and angry? As far as we can tell, the answer is no. The "good" moms we watch either don't get angry or they don't let us know they're angry. Watching such folks can leave us frustrated and guilt-ridden regarding our own tempers.

Paul writes to those of us who struggle with anger in Ephesians 4:26. He says, "In your anger..." This little phrase packs a powerful punch because it acknowledges that it's impossible to completely avoid anger. God's unmistakably clear, inspired Word recognizes that anger is an inevitable human emotion.

But then Paul ties this little phrase to a command: "Do not sin." When we acknowledge our anger, we can face it without fear. We can separate ourselves with a "time-out" until we gain control. We can express our feelings in careful words that take personal ownership of the emotion.

What should you do with anger? First, accept its inevitability. Then, don't deny it. Use your anger constructively to change situations without destroying people. Be angry, but don't sin. Then you'll be good, and angry.

ASKING FOR HELP

Jesus said, "Ask and it will be given to you; seek and you will find; knock and the door will be opened to you. For everyone who asks receives; he who seeks finds; and to him who knocks, the door will be opened."

LUKE 11:9–10

"Call to me and I will answer you and tell you great and unsearchable things you do not know," says the LORD.

JEREMIAH 33:3

Everyone who calls
    on the name of the LORD
will be saved.

JOEL 2:32

"Call upon me in the day of trouble;
    I will deliver you, and you will honor me,"
declares the LORD.

PSALM 50:15

The LORD is near to all who call on him,
    to all who call on him in truth.
He fulfills the desires of those who fear him;
    he hears their cry and saves them.

PSALM 145:18–19

Carry each other's burdens, and in this way you will fulfill the law of Christ.

GALATIANS 6:2

Two are better than one,
    because they have a good return for their work:
If one falls down,
    his friend can help him up.

ECCLESIASTES 4:9–10

Jesus said, "The harvest is plentiful, but the workers are few. Ask the Lord of the harvest, therefore, to send out workers into his harvest field."

LUKE 10:2

Moses' father-in-law replied, "What you are doing is not good. You and these people who come to you will only wear yourselves out. The work is too heavy for you; you cannot handle it alone. … Select capable men from all the people—men who fear God, … and appoint them as officials over thousands, hundreds, fifties and tens. Have them serve as judges for the people at all times, but have them bring every difficult case to you; the simple cases they can decide themselves. That will make your load lighter, because they will share it with

11

you. If you do this and God so commands, you will be able to stand the strain, and all these people will go home satisfied." Moses listened to his father-in-law and did everything he said.

EXODUS 18:17–18, 21–24

He tends his flock like a shepherd:
    He gathers the lambs in his arms
and carries them close to his heart;
    he gently leads those that have young.

ISAIAH 40:11

Let us ... approach the throne of grace with confidence, so that we may receive mercy and find grace to help us in our time of need.

HEBREWS 4:16

In my distress I called to the LORD,
    and he answered me. ...
I called for help,
    and you listened to my cry.

JONAH 2:2

Carol Kuykendall and Elisa Morgan surveyed some 1,000 moms about their needs. To the question, "What do you need most, Mom?" they responded:

A nanny
A housekeeper
A secretary
Another set of arms
To get organized
Help

We can easily blurt out confessions like these, but when it comes down to everyday life, most of us have a tough time actually asking for help. Griping seems to come more easily.

Perhaps we feel that asking for help is a sign of weakness. Or maybe we feel guilty about asking for help. Moms are supposed to be able to fix whatever is broken or hurt, and do it better than anyone else.

The toughest—but most important—question we may ever have to ask is, "Will you help me?" If Moses couldn't handle all the needs of the Israelites alone, why do we think we can handle all the needs of those around us without help? So, Mom, swallow hard and ask the question, "Will you help me?"

ATTITUDE

Your attitude should be the same as that of Christ Jesus:

Who, being in very nature God,
  did not consider equality with God something to
    be grasped,
but made himself nothing,
  taking the very nature of a servant,
  being made in human likeness.
And being found in appearance as a man,
  he humbled himself
  and became obedient to death—
    even death on a cross!
Therefore God exalted him to the highest place
  and gave him the name that is above every name,
that at the name of Jesus every knee should bow,
  in heaven and on earth and under the earth
and every tongue confess that Jesus Christ is Lord,
  to the glory of God the Father.

PHILIPPIANS 2:5–11

Guard your heart,
  for it is the wellspring of life.

PROVERBS 4:23

ATTITUDE

*Let us … make every effort to do what leads to peace
and to mutual edification.*
ROMANS 14:19

What does the LORD require of you?
To act justly and to love mercy
and to walk humbly with your God.
MICAH 6:8

*You were taught, with regard to your former way of life,
to put off your old self, which is being corrupted by its
deceitful desires; to be made new in the attitude of your
minds; and to put on the new self, created to be like
God in true righteousness and holiness.*
EPHESIANS 4:22–24

*Let the word of Christ dwell in you richly as you teach
and admonish one another with all wisdom, and as
you sing psalms, hymns and spiritual songs with gratitude in your hearts to God. And whatever you do,
whether in word or deed, do it all in the name of the
Lord Jesus.*
COLOSSIANS 3:16–17

Whoever claims to live in God must walk as Jesus did.
1 JOHN 2:6

I try to please everybody in every way. For I am not seeking my own good but the good of many, so that they may be saved.
1 CORINTHIANS 10:33

Jesus said, "Whoever wants to become great among you must be your servant, and whoever wants to be first must be your slave—just as the Son of Man did not come to be served, but to serve, and to give his life as a ransom for many."
MATTHEW 20:26–28

Nobody should seek his own good, but the good of others.
1 CORINTHIANS 10:24

Each of us should please his neighbor for his good, to build him up.
ROMANS 15:2

Jesus said, "The greatest among you will be your servant. For whoever exalts himself will be humbled, and whoever humbles himself will be exalted."
MATTHEW 23:11–12

Jesus said, "In everything, do to others what you would have them do to you."
MATTHEW 7:12

DEVOTIONAL THOUGHT
ON ATTITUDE

We take out the trash. We wash the dishes and clear off the kitchen counters. We even vacuum on occasion. We carefully attend to the condition of our homes in order to keep them off the "disaster area" list. But how much attention do we give to our hearts?

When the Bible says that the heart is to be guarded because it is the wellspring of life, it means that it is from our hearts that the rest of our attitudes get their cue. Depressed? Check the contentment quotient of your heart. Feel like griping? Once again, review your heart and then you'll know why.

Rather than cleaning up the outer edges of our lives, we're wiser to pay attention to the deeper parts of ourselves. Running the vacuum cleaner through a few ventricles, we may discover a layer of dissatisfaction, of envy, or even of anger that we've stuffed out of sight.

There's no use trying to paste on a happy face or a good attitude to show in public if our hearts are cluttered with hidden issues. What's stuffed down in our hearts will sooner or later spill over into our days with our children, our neighbors, our co-workers, and God.

Everything that was written in the past was written to teach us, so that through endurance and the encouragement of the Scriptures we might have hope.

ROMANS 15:4

The word of God is living and active. Sharper than any double-edged sword, it penetrates even to dividing soul and spirit, joints and marrow; it judges the thoughts and attitudes of the heart.

HEBREWS 4:12

Like newborn babies, crave pure spiritual milk, so that by it you may grow up in your salvation.

1 PETER 2:2

Oh, how I love your law, LORD!
    I meditate on it all day long.

PSALM 119:97

Let us discern for ourselves what is right;
    let us learn together what is good.

JOB 34:4

Grow in the grace and knowledge of our Lord and Savior Jesus Christ. To him be glory both now and forever!

2 PETER 3:18

BIBLE STUDY

*My purpose is that they may be encouraged in heart
and united in love, so that they may have the full riches
of complete understanding, in order that they may
know the mystery of God, namely, Christ, in whom are
hidden all the treasures of wisdom and knowledge.*

COLOSSIANS 2:2–3

Your statutes are my heritage forever, O LORD;
>   they are the joy of my heart.

PSALM 119:111

*This is my prayer: that your love may abound more
and more in knowledge and depth of insight, so that
you may be able to discern what is best and may be
pure and blameless until the day of Christ.*

PHILIPPIANS 1:9–10

I have more insight than all my teachers,
>   for I meditate on your statutes, O LORD.

I have more understanding than the elders,
>   for I obey your precepts.

I have kept my feet from every evil path
>   so that I might obey your word.

I have not departed from your laws,
>   for you yourself have taught me.

BIBLE STUDY

How sweet are your words to my taste, O LORD,
   sweeter than honey to my mouth!
I gain understanding from your precepts;
   therefore I hate every wrong path.
Your word is a lamp to my feet
   and a light for my path.

PSALM 119:99–105

Every word of God is flawless;
   he is a shield to those who take refuge in him.

PROVERBS 30:5

The law of the LORD is perfect,
   reviving the soul.
The statutes of the LORD are trustworthy,
   making wise the simple.
The precepts of the LORD are right,
   giving joy to the heart.
The commands of the LORD are radiant,
   giving light to the eyes.
The fear of the LORD is pure,
   enduring forever.
The ordinances of the LORD are sure
   and altogether righteous.
They are more precious than gold,

than much pure gold;
they are sweeter than honey,
than honey from the comb.
By them is your servant warned;
in keeping them there is great reward.

PSALM 19:7–11

When [the king] takes the throne of his kingdom, he is to write for himself on a scroll a copy of this law, taken from that of the priests. ... It is to be with him, and he is to read it all the days of his life so that he may learn to revere the LORD his God and follow carefully all the words of this law and these decrees.

DEUTERONOMY 17:18–19

Continue in what you have learned and have become convinced of, because you know those from whom you learned it, and how from infancy you have known the holy Scriptures, which are able to make you wise for salvation through faith in Christ Jesus.

2 TIMOTHY 3:14–15

The unfolding of your words gives light, O God;
it gives understanding to the simple.

PSALM 119:130

BIBLE STUDY

I remember your ancient laws, O LORD,
and I find comfort in them.

PSALM 119:52

Do not let this Book of the Law depart from your mouth; meditate on it day and night, so that you may be careful to do everything written in it. Then you will be prosperous and successful.

JOSHUA 1:8

When your words came, I ate them;
they were my joy and my heart's delight,
for I bear your name,
O LORD God Almighty.

JEREMIAH 15:16

Jesus said, "Blessed ... are those who hear the word of God and obey it."

LUKE 11:28

You're unleashing unkind words at your husband when suddenly into your mind comes a phrase: "Do not let any unwholesome talk come out of your mouths." Where did this come from?

You're flipping through a home decorating magazine when another phrase comes into your thoughts: "I have learned the secret of being content in any and every situation." Amazing!

These kinds of experiences illustrate what Paul means in 2 Timothy 3:16. The Word of God is living. What we read in the Bible are his exact, actual words, spoken through a human instrument, passed down orally and then finally, written in historical narratives, literature or letter form. God's words continue to speak even today to all who read and listen.

In 2 Timothy 3:16, Paul stresses four functions of the living Word, the Bible:

Teaching: It imparts to us information about truth
            and God.

Rebuking: It tells us when we are wrong.

Correcting: It redirects us when we stray.

Training: It prepares us for each next step along
            the pathway of becoming like him.

The Bible is God's actual, living Word. He speaks when we read it. And he speaks again in our day-to-day experience when he helps us recall what he says.

CHILDREN

Sons are a heritage from the LORD,
  children a reward from him.
Like arrows in the hands of a warrior
  are sons born in one's youth.

PSALM 127:3–4

The LORD your God will make you most prosperous in
all the work of your hands and in the fruit of your
womb.

DEUTERONOMY 30:9

Parents are the pride of their children.

PROVERBS 17:6

May the LORD make you increase,
  both you and your children.
May you be blessed by the LORD,
  the Maker of heaven and earth.

PSALM 115:14–15

Jesus said, "Let the little children come to me, and do
not hinder them, for the kingdom of heaven belongs to
such as these."

MATTHEW 19:14

"Do not forget the things your eyes have seen or let them slip from your heart as long as you live. Teach them to your children and to their children after them," says the LORD.

DEUTERONOMY 4:9

Train a child in the way he should go,
    and when he is old he will not turn from it.

PROVERBS 22:6

All your sons will be taught by the LORD,
    and great will be your children's peace.

ISAIAH 54:13

Do not exasperate your children; instead, bring them up in the training and instruction of the Lord.

EPHESIANS 6:4

God will love you and bless you and increase your numbers. He will bless the fruit of your womb.

DEUTERONOMY 7:13

Fathers tell their children about your faithfulness,
O LORD.

ISAIAH 38:19

CHILDREN

Jesus said, "A woman giving birth to a child has pain because her time has come; but when her baby is born she forgets the anguish because of her joy that a child is born into the world."

JOHN 16:21

I prayed for this child, and the LORD has granted me what I asked of him. So now I give him to the LORD.

1 SAMUEL 1:27–28

The disciples came to Jesus and asked, "Who is the greatest in the kingdom of heaven?" He called a little child and had him stand among them. And he said: "I tell you the truth, unless you change and become like little children, you will never enter the kingdom of heaven. Therefore, whoever humbles himself like this child is the greatest in the kingdom of heaven. And whoever welcomes a little child like this in my name welcomes me."

MATTHEW 18:1–5

I have no greater joy than to hear that my children are walking in the truth.

3 JOHN 4

DEVOTIONAL THOUGHT
ON CHILDREN

We rock gently, back and forth, back and forth. Our baby nuzzles in our neck, breath hot on our skin. So soft. So sweet.

Carefully, we rise and pad across the carpet to the crib. We ease our little one down on the soft flannel sheet. Our baby. Our precious child. A humming melody begins deep within us: "Jesus loves you this I know…" we sing to our baby as we softly steal away and out of the room.

Where did this love come from? How did we learn to love this way?

Zephaniah pictures God quieting his child Israel and singing over it with love. Perhaps we learn child-love from the Parent who has loved us so well, who quiets us with his love, who rejoices over us with singing.

Let us not become weary in doing good, for at the proper time we will reap a harvest if we do not give up.
GALATIANS 6:9

Be strong and do not give up, for your work will be rewarded.
2 CHRONICLES 15:7

Commit your way to the LORD;
    trust in him and he will do this:
He will make your righteousness
    shine like the dawn,
        the justice of your cause like the noonday sun.
PSALM 37:5–6

Serve wholeheartedly, as if you were serving the LORD, not men, because you know that the LORD will reward everyone for whatever good he does.
EPHESIANS 6:7–8

"I will give them singleness of heart and action, so that they will always fear me for their own good and the good of their children after them. I will make an everlasting covenant with them: I will never stop doing good to them, and I will inspire them to fear me, so

*that they will never turn away from me," declares the
LORD.*
JEREMIAH 32:39–40

*Your hearts must be fully committed to the LORD our
God, to live by his decrees and obey his commands.*
1 KINGS 8:61

Place me like a seal over your heart,
    like a seal on your arm;
for love is as strong as death.
SONG OF SONGS 8:6

*Anyone who runs ahead and does not continue in the
teaching of Christ does not have God; whoever contin-
ues in the teaching has both the Father and the Son.*
2 JOHN 9

*Never be lacking in zeal, but keep your spiritual fervor,
serving the Lord.*
ROMANS 12:11

*Jesus said, "Whoever acknowledges me before men, I
will also acknowledge him before my Father in
heaven."*
MATTHEW 10:32

Jesus said, "I am coming soon. Hold on to what you have, so that no one will take your crown."
REVELATION 3:11

Hold on to the good. ... May God himself, the God of peace, sanctify you through and through. May your whole spirit, soul and body be kept blameless at the coming of our Lord Jesus Christ.
1 THESSALONIANS 5:21, 23

Nebuchadnezzar said, "Praise be to the God of Shadrach, Meshach and Abednego, who has sent his angel and rescued his servants! They trusted in him and defied the king's command and were willing to give up their lives rather than serve or worship any god except their own God."
DANIEL 3:28

Cling to what is good. ... Be devoted to one another in ... love.
ROMANS 12:9–10

I press on toward the goal to win the prize for which God has called me heavenward in Christ Jesus.
PHILIPPIANS 3:14

A friend is having an affair. A neighbor stretches the truth on an insurance claim. A loved one swears in front of the children. Sins of all kinds are all around us—and inside us. How can we break free from them and be distinctive people in Christ?

Daniel disregarded the popular beliefs of his day and lived instead by God's standards (see Daniel 1).

The "Daniel" woman doesn't walk out on her husband. She doesn't hang up on her mother. She doesn't ignore the needs of her neighbor. She doesn't insist on playing the game of life by her own rules, but rather chooses to play consistently, obediently, sometimes even painfully, by God's design. She stays committed to those around her. She recognizes and respects the bonds of a pledge, whether to a husband, a child or her God.

In our day, avoiding consequences and ignoring promises are all too common, but the woman who stands by her commitment and fights for healthy relationships is a "Daniel" woman: a distinctive person in Christ.

May the words of my mouth
and the meditation of my heart
be pleasing in your sight, O LORD.

PSALM 19:14

*Do not let any unwholesome talk come out of your
mouths, but only what is helpful for building others up
according to their needs.*

EPHESIANS 4:29

From the fruit of his lips a man enjoys good things.

PROVERBS 13:2

*Confess your sins to each other and pray for each other
so that you may be healed.*

JAMES 5:16

The mouth of the righteous man utters wisdom,
and his tongue speaks what is just.
The law of his God is in his heart;
his feet do not slip.

PSALM 37:30–31

The tongue of the righteous is choice silver.

PROVERBS 10:20

From the fruit of his mouth
a man's stomach is filled;
with the harvest from his lips he is satisfied.

PROVERBS 18:20

The tongue that brings healing is a tree of life.

PROVERBS 15:4

A wise man's heart guides his mouth,
and his lips promote instruction.
Pleasant words are a honeycomb,
sweet to the soul and healing to the bones.

PROVERBS 16:23–24

*Speak to one another with psalms, hymns and spiritual
songs. Sing and make music in your heart to the Lord,
always giving thanks to God the Father for everything,
in the name of our Lord Jesus Christ.*

EPHESIANS 5:19–20

*Through Jesus, therefore, let us continually offer to God
a sacrifice of praise—the fruit of lips that confess his
name.*

HEBREWS 13:15

A word aptly spoken
    is like apples of gold in settings of silver.

PROVERBS 25:11

LORD, who may dwell in your sanctuary?
    Who may live on your holy hill?...
[The one] who speaks the truth from his heart
    and has no slander on his tongue,
who does his neighbor no wrong
    and casts no slur on his fellowman.

PSALM 15:1–3

The Sovereign LORD has given me
    an instructed tongue,
    to know the word that sustains the weary.

ISAIAH 50:4

Truthful lips endure forever.

PROVERBS 12:19

We all stumble in many ways. If anyone is never at fault in what he says, he is a perfect man, able to keep his whole body in check.

JAMES 3:2

Set a guard over my mouth, O LORD;
keep watch over the door of my lips.

PSALM 141:3

A truthful witness gives honest testimony.

PROVERBS 12:17

*Always be prepared to give an answer to everyone who
asks you to give the reason for the hope that you have.
But do this with gentleness and respect.*

1 PETER 3:15

*Speaking the truth in love, we will in all things grow
up into him who is the Head, that is, Christ.*

EPHESIANS 4:15

He who guards his lips guards his life.

PROVERBS 13:3

*Let your conversation be always full of grace, sea-
soned with salt, so that you may know how to answer
everyone.*

COLOSSIANS 4:6

Whoever of you loves life
    and desires to see many good days,
keep your tongue from evil
    and your lips from speaking lies.

PSALM 34:12–13

An honest answer
    is like a kiss on the lips.

PROVERBS 24:26

The tongue of the wise commends knowledge.

PROVERBS 15:2

If anyone speaks, he should do it as one speaking the very words of God.

1 PETER 4:11

DEVOTIONAL THOUGHT ON COMMUNICATION

To a large degree, our children become what we tell them they are. If we tell our children they are clumsy, forgetful or stupid, they will be clumsy, forgetful or stupid. How we react to our children's shortcomings—when they spill their breakfast cereal, when they leave their assignment for class at home, or when they return from a friend's house an hour late—determines what they will think of themselves and what they will become.

In Genesis 49, Jacob blesses each of his sons, speaking "words of becoming" over them. We can do the same. We can start feeding our children praise in the ordinary moments of our days. Give it like a vitamin supplement at each meal. Offer it for midday snacks. Serve it for a substantial dessert. No matter what the age of our children, it's never too late to include the all-important nutrient of affirmation in their diet.

At two, twelve or twenty-two, what we tell them they are, our children will become. What we say is what we'll get.

I am convinced that neither death nor life, neither angels nor demons, neither the present nor the future, nor any powers, neither height nor depth, nor anything else in all creation, will be able to separate us from the love of God that is in Christ Jesus our Lord.

ROMANS 8:38–39

Do not throw away your confidence; it will be richly rewarded.

HEBREWS 10:35

I am still confident of this:
> I will see the goodness of the LORD
> in the land of the living.

PSALM 27:13

The effect of righteousness will be quietness and
> confidence forever.

ISAIAH 32:17

We say with confidence, "The Lord is my helper; I will not be afraid. What can man do to me?"

HEBREWS 13:6

The LORD is my light and my salvation—
> whom shall I fear?

CONFIDENCE

The LORD is the stronghold of my life—
  of whom shall I be afraid? ...
Though an army besiege me,
  my heart will not fear;
though war break out against me,
  even then will I be confident.

PSALM 27:1, 3

Let us ... approach the throne of grace with confidence,
so that we may receive mercy and find grace to help us
in our time of need.

HEBREWS 4:16

I know that my Redeemer lives,
  and that in the end
he will stand upon the earth.

JOB 19:25

God alone is my rock and my salvation;
  he is my fortress, I will never be shaken.

PSALM 62:2

Jesus said, "My sheep listen to my voice; I know them,
and they follow me. I give them eternal life, and they
shall never perish; no one can snatch them out of my

hand. My Father, who has given them to me, is greater than all; no one can snatch them out of my Father's hand."

JOHN 10:27–29

I am not ashamed, because I know whom I have believed, and am convinced that God is able to guard what I have entrusted to him for that day.

2 TIMOTHY 1:12

I can do everything through Christ who gives me strength.

PHILIPPIANS 4:13

God who began a good work in you will carry it on to completion until the day of Christ Jesus.

PHILIPPIANS 1:6

We have come to share in Christ if we hold firmly till the end the confidence we had at first.

HEBREWS 3:14

This is the confidence we have in approaching God: that if we ask anything according to his will, he hears us.

1 JOHN 5:14

CONFIDENCE

If our hearts do not condemn us, we have confidence before God.

1 JOHN 3:21

The LORD will be your confidence
and will keep your foot from being snared.

PROVERBS 3:26

The eternal God is your refuge,
and underneath are the everlasting arms.

DEUTERONOMY 33:27

The LORD is my rock, my fortress and my deliverer;
my God is my rock, in whom I take refuge.
He is my shield and the
horn of my salvation, my stronghold.

PSALM 18:2

You are my hiding place; O LORD,
you will protect me from trouble
and surround me with songs of deliverance.

PSALM 32:7

The name of the LORD is a strong tower;
the righteous run to it and are safe.

PROVERBS 18:10

Blessed is the man who trusts in the LORD,
     whose confidence is in him.

JEREMIAH 17:7

*I eagerly expect and hope that I will in no way be
ashamed, but will have sufficient courage so that now
as always Christ will be exalted in my body, whether by
life or by death.*

PHILIPPIANS 1:20

*You will not have to fight this battle. Take up your
positions; stand firm and see the deliverance the
LORD will give you. ... Do not be afraid; do not be
discouraged.*

2 CHRONICLES 20:17

*The Lord said to me, "My grace is sufficient for you, for
my power is made perfect in weakness." Therefore I will
boast all the more gladly about my weaknesses, so that
Christ's power may rest on me.*

2 CORINTHIANS 12:9

_____

Eagerly I've asked God to take charge of my children. Out of fear that I might "ruin" them, I hand them over to him.

But as I give my children to God, I often hear him ask, "Do you really trust me with your children? Do you trust me to get them to school safely?"

"Yes!" I respond.

"Do you believe that I can guide them through an illness?"

"Of course!"

"How about deciding if they will marry—and who?"

"Better you than I!" I say.

"Then do you trust me to select the very best mother for your children and for who I want them to become?"

We can be the mothers our children need because God divinely chose us for the job. Don't doubt it. He knows what he is doing. And aren't we glad!

May the God who gives endurance and encouragement give you a spirit of unity among yourselves as you follow Christ Jesus, so that with one heart and mouth you may glorify the God and Father of our Lord Jesus Christ.
ROMANS 15:5–6

Agree with one another so that there may be no divisions among you.
1 CORINTHIANS 1:10

Hatred stirs up dissension,
    but love covers over all wrongs.
PROVERBS 10:12

Make every effort to keep the unity of the Spirit.
EPHESIANS 4:3

Make sure that nobody pays back wrong for wrong.
1 THESSALONIANS 5:15

Do not be overcome by evil, but overcome evil with good.
ROMANS 12:21

A fool shows his annoyance at once,
    but a prudent man overlooks an insult.
PROVERBS 12:16

CONFLICT

It is to a man's honor to avoid strife.

PROVERBS 20:3

Starting a quarrel is like breaching a dam;
    so drop the matter before a dispute breaks out.

PROVERBS 17:14

Pride only breeds quarrels,
    but wisdom is found in those who take advice.

PROVERBS 13:10

A gentle answer turns away wrath.

PROVERBS 15:1

Do not be quickly provoked in your spirit.

ECCLESIASTES 7:9

There should be no division in the body, but that its parts should have equal concern for each other. If one part suffers, every part suffers with it; if one part is honored, every part rejoices with it.

1 CORINTHIANS 12:25–26

Jesus said, "I pray also for those who will believe in me through [my disciples'] message, that all of them may be one, Father, just as you are in me and I am in you. ...

*May they be brought to complete unity to let the world
know that you sent me."*

JOHN 17:20–21, 23

He who pursues righteousness and love
    finds life, prosperity and honor.

PROVERBS 21:21

DEVOTIONAL THOUGHT ON CONFLICT

Conflict is inevitable. Even the most loving of couples and devoted of friends will find themselves pulled apart by the differences of background and belief—disagreements over finances, child-rearing and household chores. Such moments are dangerous. When emotions run high, the verbal arrows fly and lodge in places where they were never aimed.

We can avoid the danger of conflict by following one simple guideline: Don't attack people, attack problems. Instead of focusing on the person with whom we're in conflict, we can direct our attention toward the problem that is separating us. Here are several helpful steps:

- *Write your feelings down before you say them.* Pour out your feelings on the safety of paper.

- *Define the problem.* Start with several sentences and eventually work your way down to a word or two that defines the problem.

- *Communicate the problem carefully.* Erase exaggerations from your vocabulary. Resist saying "You never" or "You always." Avoid accusations and name-calling.

Malachi 3:16 says the Israelites "talked with each other" in order to find resolution to their conflict. When we train ourselves to attack our problems rather than people, we work our way toward healthy resolution without leaving casualties in our wake.

The boundary lines have fallen
    for me in pleasant places;
        surely I have a delightful inheritance.

PSALM 16:6

Better a meal of vegetables where there is love
    than a fattened calf with hatred.

PROVERBS 15:17

*Each one should retain the place in life that the Lord
assigned to him and to which God has called him.*

1 CORINTHIANS 7:17

Be still before the LORD and wait patiently for him;
    do not fret when men succeed in their ways,
    when they carry out their wicked schemes.
Refrain from anger and turn from wrath;
    do not fret—it leads only to evil.
For evil men will be cut off,
    but those who hope in the LORD
    will inherit the land.

PSALM 37:7–9

*Go, eat your food with gladness, and drink your wine
with a joyful heart, for it is now that God favors what
you do.*

ECCLESIASTES 9:7

Better the little that the righteous have
    than the wealth of many wicked;
for the power of the wicked will be broken,
    but the LORD upholds the righteous.

PSALM 37:16–17

The cheerful heart has a continual feast.

PROVERBS 15:15

*Better one handful with tranquillity than two handfuls
with toil and chasing after the wind.*

ECCLESIASTES 4:6

A happy heart makes the face cheerful.

PROVERBS 15:13

Give me neither poverty nor riches,
    but give me only my daily bread.

PROVERBS 30:8

Better a little with the fear of the LORD
    than great wealth with turmoil.

PROVERBS 15:16

Keep your lives free from the love of money and be content with what you have, because God has said, "Never will I leave you; never will I forsake you."

HEBREWS 13:5

Better a little with righteousness
  than much gain with injustice.

PROVERBS 16:8

*Godliness with contentment is great gain. For we
brought nothing into the world, and we can take nothing out of it. But if we have food and clothing, we will
be content with that.*

1 TIMOTHY 6:6–8

Better a dry crust with peace and quiet
  than a house full of feasting, with strife.

PROVERBS 17:1

*I have learned to be content whatever the circum-
stances. I know what it is to be in need, and I know
what it is to have plenty. I have learned the secret of
being content in any and every situation, whether
well fed or hungry, whether living in plenty or in
want. I can do everything through Christ who gives
me strength.*

PHILIPPIANS 4:11–13

DEVOTIONAL THOUGHT
ON CONTENTMENT

I don't want this couch—I want a leather one! I don't like this house—I want a bigger one! I'm not satisfied with my husband—I want hers! While such words rarely escape our lips, the thoughts behind them are regular enough.

So too with the Israelites who griped and grumbled to God during their wanderings in the wilderness. They fussed at God because they didn't think they had enough food. Then they raised their fists at him because all he provided was manna and they wanted meat. They griped about not being in the Promised Land when they were in the desert. And yet, it was in the desert that God offered unique and tangible demonstrations of his presence: a pillar of fire, a cloud of presence, manna and quail from the sky.

How like the Israelites we are! We say we want certain things from God and yet when we have them, we look longingly back at the way things were before, never fully satisfied. So what's our beef with God? Do we want the Promised Land or his presence in our life?

EMOTIONS

The mind controlled by the Spirit is life and peace.
ROMANS 8:6

Put on the new self, which is being renewed in knowledge in the image of its Creator.
COLOSSIANS 3:10

Do not conform any longer to the pattern of this world, but be transformed by the renewing of your mind.
ROMANS 12:2

"I will give you a new heart and put a new spirit in you; I will remove from you your heart of stone and give you a heart of flesh. And I will put my Spirit in you and move you to follow my decrees and be careful to keep my laws," says the LORD.
EZEKIEL 36:26–27

Search me, O God, and know my heart;
    test me and know my anxious thoughts.
PSALM 139:23

All my longings lie open before you, O LORD;
    my sighing is not hidden from you. …
Come quickly to help me,
    O Lord my Savior.
PSALM 38:9, 22

Our mouths were filled with laughter,
    our tongues with songs of joy.
PSALM 126:2

How long must I wrestle with my thoughts
    and every day have sorrow in my heart? ...
But I trust in your unfailing love, O LORD;
    my heart rejoices in your salvation.
I will sing to the LORD,
    for he has been good to me.
PSALM 13:2, 5–6

I pour out my complaint before God;
    before him I tell my trouble.
When my spirit grows faint within me,
    it is you, O LORD, who know my way.
PSALM 142:2–3

I will praise the LORD, who counsels me;
    even at night my heart instructs me.
I have set the LORD always before me.
    Because he is at my right hand,
    I will not be shaken.
Therefore my heart is glad and my tongue rejoices.
PSALM 16:7–9

Is anyone happy? Let him sing songs of praise.
JAMES 5:13

May the righteous be glad
  and rejoice before God;
  may they be happy and joyful.
PSALM 68:3

Why are you downcast, O my soul?
  Why so disturbed within me?
Put your hope in God,
  for I will yet praise him,
  my Savior and my God.
PSALM 43:5

Whether experienced as "Monday morning blues," "rainy day feelings," "winter blahs," or just "down days," folks struggle with bouts of depression. Moms are no exception.

Depression is generally defined as discouragement resulting from the experience of loss or internalized anger. We who walk through its valley of shadows tend to consider ourselves abnormal and even condemn our pessimistic periods, seeing them as detours from faith.

Many Christian psychologists and theologians are attempting to change this negative view. The truth is that life is tough. Adjusting to it is hard. While we are immeasurably strengthened through our relationship with Christ, we will still face difficult adjustments in life. In some cases, we may need the help of a trained professional to successfully travel through deep valleys.

But on other days, we do well to remind ourselves of the truth of Ecclesiastes 7:14: "When times are good, be happy; but when times are bad, consider: God has made the one as well as the other." There are fifty-two Monday mornings each year. On your next blue Monday, take the advice of the writer of Ecclesiastes: stop and "consider."

May our Lord Jesus Christ himself and God our Father, who loved us and by his grace gave us eternal encouragement and good hope, encourage your hearts and strengthen you in every good deed and word.

2 THESSALONIANS 2:16–17

The LORD is good to those whose hope is in him,
    to the one who seeks him.

LAMENTATIONS 3:25

God, who has called you into fellowship with his Son Jesus Christ our Lord, is faithful.

1 CORINTHIANS 1:9

    Though I have fallen, I will rise.
Though I sit in darkness,
    the LORD will be my light.

MICAH 7:8

May the God who gives endurance and encouragement give you a spirit of unity among yourselves as you follow Christ Jesus, so that with one heart and mouth you may glorify the God and Father of our Lord Jesus Christ.

ROMANS 15:5–6

This I call to mind
   and therefore I have hope:
Because of the LORD'S great love we are not
            consumed,
   for his compassions never fail.
They are new every morning;
   great is your faithfulness.

LAMENTATIONS 3:21–23

Your love has given me great joy and encouragement.

PHILEMON 7

Praise be to the God and Father of our Lord Jesus
Christ, the Father of compassion and the God of all
comfort, who comforts us in all our troubles, so that we
can comfort those in any trouble with the comfort we
ourselves have received from God. For just as the suffer-
ings of Christ flow over into our lives, so also through
Christ our comfort overflows.

2 CORINTHIANS 1:3–5

Everything that was written in the past was written to
teach us, so that through endurance and the encourage-
ment of the Scriptures we might have hope.

ROMANS 15:4

The LORD is my rock, my fortress and my deliverer;
  my God is my rock, in whom I take refuge.
PSALM 18:2

Encourage one another and build each other up.
1 THESSALONIANS 5:11

You are a shield around me, O LORD;
  you bestow glory on me and lift up my head.
PSALM 3:3

The LORD is my strength and my song;
  he has become my salvation.
He is my God, and I will praise him.
EXODUS 15:2

Cast your cares on the LORD
  and he will sustain you;
  he will never let the righteous fall.
PSALM 55:22

*"For I know the plans I have for you," declares the
LORD, "plans to prosper you and not to harm you, plans
to give you a hope and a future."*
JEREMIAH 29:11

How desperately we as moms need a refuge, a place of retreat and safety when we have failed. When we have lost our last shred of control and hollered at our treasured child. When we selfishly refused to help our husband because we wanted him to handle it.

God is that safe place in such moments. He has set himself apart for us so that he is available to meet our needs whenever, whatever, they are.

What is it you need today? Forgiveness? Hope? Encouragement? Strength to begin again? Why not go to your refuge? Go to God.

FAITH

Faith is being sure of what we hope for and certain of what we do not see.

HEBREWS 11:1

Faith comes from hearing the message, and the message is heard through the word of Christ.

ROMANS 10:17

Abram believed the LORD, and he credited it to him as righteousness.

GENESIS 15:6

Let us fix our eyes on Jesus, the author and perfecter of our faith, who for the joy set before him endured the cross, scorning its shame, and sat down at the right hand of the throne of God.

HEBREWS 12:2

"Have faith in God," Jesus said. "I tell you the truth, if anyone says to this mountain, 'Go, throw yourself into the sea,' and does not doubt in his heart but believes that what he says will happen, it will be done for him. Therefore I tell you, whatever you ask for in prayer, believe that you have received it, and it will be yours."

MARK 11:22–24

FAITH

We live by faith, not by sight.
2 CORINTHIANS 5:7

By faith we understand that the universe was formed at God's command, so that what is seen was not made out of what was visible.
HEBREWS 11:3

Without faith it is impossible to please God.
HEBREWS 11:6

[Trials] have come so that your faith—of greater worth than gold, which perishes even though refined by fire— may be proved genuine and may result in praise, glory and honor when Jesus Christ is revealed.
1 PETER 1:7

A woman ... came up behind Jesus and touched the edge of his cloak. She said to herself, "If I only touch his cloak, I will be healed." Jesus turned and saw her. "Take heart, daughter," he said, "your faith has healed you." And the woman was healed from that moment.
MATTHEW 9:20–22

By faith Abraham, even though he was past age—and Sarah herself was barren—was enabled to become a

*father because he considered God faithful who had
made the promise.*
HEBREWS 11:11

*In his great mercy God has given us new birth into a
living hope through the resurrection of Jesus Christ from
the dead, and into an inheritance that can never perish,
spoil or fade—kept in heaven for you, who through
faith are shielded by God's power until the coming of
the salvation that is ready to be revealed in the last
time.*
1 PETER 1:3–5

*Yet to all who received God, to those who believed in his
name, he gave the right to become children of God—
children born not of natural descent, nor of human
decision or a husband's will, but born of God.*
JOHN 1:12–13

*By faith Moses, when he had grown up, refused to be
known as the son of Pharaoh's daughter. He chose to
be mistreated along with the people of God rather
than to enjoy the pleasures of sin for a short time. He
regarded disgrace for the sake of Christ as of greater
value than the treasures of Egypt, because he was*

FAITH

looking ahead to his reward.
HEBREWS 11:24–26

Jesus said, "My Father's will is that everyone who looks to the Son and believes in him shall have eternal life, and I will raise him up at the last day."
JOHN 6:40

Since we have been justified through faith, we have peace with God through our Lord Jesus Christ.
ROMANS 5:1

For it is by grace you have been saved, through faith— and this not from yourselves, it is the gift of God—not by works, so that no one can boast.
EPHESIANS 2:8–9

Jesus said, "I tell you the truth, whoever hears my word and believes him who sent me has eternal life and will not be condemned; he has crossed over from death to life."
JOHN 5:24

Jesus declared, "I am the bread of life. He who comes to me will never go hungry, and he who believes in me will never be thirsty."
JOHN 6:35

FAITH

This righteousness from God comes through faith in Jesus Christ to all who believe. There is no difference, for all have sinned and fall short of the glory of God, and are justified freely by his grace through the redemption that came by Christ Jesus.

ROMANS 3:22–24

If you confess with your mouth, "Jesus is Lord," and believe in your heart that God raised him from the dead, you will be saved. For it is with your heart that you believe and are justified, and it is with your mouth that you confess and are saved.

ROMANS 10:9–10

Mothers face mountains all the time. Heaps of laundry. Mounds of applesauce on tables. Towers of wooden blocks. And the unconquered heights of potty training. How are we to respond?

Jesus tells us to respond with faith. With faith all things are possible. When we surround ourselves with proof of God's control over our days, our spirits are lifted and most mountains do, in fact, move.

And when they won't? When it's 9:30 at night and we're still stumbling through toppled blocks on our way to throw in another load of wash—what then? When the mountains don't move, we can respond with perspective, knowing that we are living in a season of life today that will change tomorrow. These mountains will pass—and others will take their place, like the mountain of trusting a teenager to drive or date, or the mountain of our child's college, career and mate decisions.

When the mountains won't move, we can hold tight to the God who is in control and let him lead us through these days, picking the path around the mountains to the other side.

A man will leave his father and mother and be united to his wife, and the two will become one flesh.
EPHESIANS 5:31

Both the one who makes men holy and those who are made holy are of the same family. So Jesus is not ashamed to call them brothers.
HEBREWS 2:11

Honor your father and mother ... that it may go well with you and that you may enjoy long life on the earth.
EPHESIANS 6:2–3

Above all, love each other deeply, because love covers over a multitude of sins.
1 PETER 4:8

As we have opportunity, let us do good to all people, especially to those who belong to the family of believers.
GALATIANS 6:10

Be devoted to one another in brotherly love. Honor one another above yourselves.
ROMANS 12:10

Train a child in the way he should go,

and when he is old he will not turn from it.
PROVERBS 22:6

A wife of noble character who can find?
    She is worth far more than rubies.
Her husband has full confidence in her
    and lacks nothing of value. ...
Her children arise and call her blessed;
    her husband also, and he praises her:
"Many women do noble things,
    but you surpass them all."
PROVERBS 31:10–11, 28–29

*Love the LORD your God with all your heart and with
all your soul and with all your strength. These com-
mandments ... are to be upon your hearts. Impress
them on your children. Talk about them when you sit
at home and when you walk along the road, when you
lie down and when you get up. Tie them as symbols on
your hands and bind them on your foreheads. Write
them on the doorframes of your houses and on your
gates.*
DEUTERONOMY 6:5–9

Jesus said, "Love one another. As I have loved you, so you must love one another."

JOHN 13:34

Let the word of Christ dwell in you richly as you teach and admonish one another with all wisdom, and as you sing psalms, hymns and spiritual songs with gratitude in your hearts to God.

COLOSSIANS 3:16

Just as each of us has one body with many members, and these members do not all have the same function, so in Christ we who are many form one body, and each member belongs to all the others.

ROMANS 12:4–5

As God's chosen people, holy and dearly loved, clothe yourselves with compassion, kindness, humility, gentleness and patience. Bear with each other and forgive whatever grievances you may have against one another. Forgive as the Lord forgave you. And over all these virtues put on love, which binds them all together in perfect unity.

COLOSSIANS 3:12–14

In times past, families were represented by coats of arms. These symbolic emblems of family ties were originally embroidered on a coat and later passed down through generations on tapestries and drawings. They depicted the outstanding characteristics and goals of a given family tribe. Animals stood for qualities like power or justice. Flowers might represent virtues. Specific colors were associated with clans and afforded immediate identification of a family.

The family coat of arms of old identified who you were and what you stood for. If you had a coat of arms for your family today, what would it communicate about your family? Is yours a tapestry woven with the fruits of love, joy, peace, patience and kindness? Do the threads of your spiritual heritage, passed down from generation to generation, show through? Does your family demonstrate a faith that expresses itself actively in the lives of those around you?

If you were to draw a coat of arms to represent the stuff of which your family is made, what would it look like?

FEAR

The LORD is my light and my salvation—
  whom shall I fear?
The LORD is the stronghold of my life—
  of whom shall I be afraid?

PSALM 27:1

The Lord will command his angels concerning you
  to guard you in all your ways;
they will lift you up in their hands,
  so that you will not strike your foot
  against a stone.
You will tread upon the lion and the cobra;
  you will trample the great lion and the serpent.
"Because he loves me," says the LORD, "I will rescue
    him;
  I will protect him, for he acknowledges my
    name."

PSALM 91:11–14

*God did not give us a spirit of timidity, but a spirit of
power.*
2 TIMOTHY 1:7

Do not fear, for I am with you;
  do not be dismayed, for I am your God.

FEAR

I will strengthen you and help you;
  I will uphold you with my righteous right hand.
ISAIAH 41:10

*Jesus said, "Do not be afraid, little flock, for your
Father has been pleased to give you the kingdom."*
LUKE 12:32

The Lord is my helper; I will not be afraid.
HEBREWS 13:6

*When the servant of the man of God got up and went
out early the next morning, an army with horses and
chariots had surrounded the city. "Oh, my lord, what
shall we do?" the servant asked. "Don't be afraid," the
prophet answered. "Those who are with us are more
than those who are with them." And Elisha prayed, "O
LORD, open his eyes so he may see." Then the LORD
opened the servant's eyes, and he looked and saw the
hills full of horses and chariots of fire all around Elisha.*
2 KINGS 6:15–17

There is no fear in love. But perfect love drives out fear.
1 JOHN 4:18

FEAR

I will say of the LORD, "He is my refuge and my
        fortress,
    my God, in whom I trust." ...
He will cover you with his feathers,
    and under his wings you will find refuge;
his faithfulness will be your shield and rampart.

PSALM 91:2, 4

God is our refuge and strength,
    an ever-present help in trouble.
Therefore we will not fear, though the earth give way
    and the mountains fall into the heart of the sea.

PSALM 46:1–2

My flesh and my heart may fail,
    but God is the strength of my heart
    and my portion forever.

PSALM 73:26

*The LORD is with you when you are with him. If you
seek him, he will be found by you.*

2 CHRONICLES 15:2

*Do not be afraid. Stand firm and you will see the
deliverance the LORD will bring you today.*

EXODUS 14:13

FEAR

Be strong and courageous, and do the work. Do not be afraid or discouraged, for the LORD God, my God, is with you. He will not fail you.

1 CHRONICLES 28:20

Though an army besiege me,
    my heart will not fear;
though war break out against me,
    even then will I be confident.

PSALM 27:3

Even though I walk
    through the valley of the shadow of death,
I will fear no evil.

PSALM 23:4

If God is for us, who can be against us?

ROMANS 8:31

The LORD is with me; I will not be afraid.
    What can man do to me?

PSALM 118:6

When I am afraid,
    I will trust in you, O LORD.

PSALM 56:3

FEAR

*Jesus said, "Peace I leave with you; my peace I give you.
I do not give to you as the world gives. Do not let your
hearts be troubled and do not be afraid."*

JOHN 14:27

*John wrote, "When I saw Christ, I fell at his feet as
though dead. Then he placed his right hand on me and
said: 'Do not be afraid. I am the First and the Last. I
am the Living One; I was dead, and behold I am alive
for ever and ever!'"*

REVELATION 1:17–18

The LORD has taken away your punishment,
    he has turned back your enemy.
The LORD, the King of Israel, is with you;
    never again will you fear any harm.

ZEPHANIAH 3:15

*You did not receive a spirit that makes you a slave
again to fear, but you received the Spirit of sonship.
And by him we cry, "Abba, Father." The Spirit himself
testifies with our spirit that we are God's children.*

ROMANS 8:15–16

DEVOTIONAL THOUGHT
ON FEAR

We ought to be thankful for some forms of fear. Fear prompts us to check on the kids in their beds when a sound wakes us at night. Fear makes us grab a child who is toddling out into the street.

Some forms of fear are healthy and provide protection. But when fear becomes the center of our lives, dictating our action or inaction, it ceases to be helpful and becomes a hindrance to our growth. When we shut ourselves away in our homes, insulating our families from the "harm" in the world, we also separate them from interaction in life as well as from the potential good they could accomplish in a world that needs the love of Christ.

In which camp do your fears fall? Does your fear serve you well by protecting you from harm? Or does it hold you and your family back from your God-given potential?

FORGIVENESS

When you were dead in your sins ... God made you alive with Christ. He forgave us all our sins, having canceled the written code, with its regulations, that was against us and that stood opposed to us; he took it away, nailing it to the cross.

COLOSSIANS 2:13–14

As far as the east is from the west, so far has God
　　removed our transgressions from us.

PSALM 103:12

"I will cleanse them from all the sin they have committed against me and will forgive all their sins of rebellion against me," says the LORD.

JEREMIAH 33:8

Bear with each other and forgive whatever grievances you may have against one another. Forgive as the Lord forgave you.

COLOSSIANS 3:13

"Come now, let us reason together,"
　　says the LORD.
"Though your sins are like scarlet,
　　they shall be as white as snow;

though they are red as crimson,
  they shall be like wool."
ISAIAH 1:18

God was reconciling the world to himself in Christ, not counting men's sins against them. And he has committed to us the message of reconciliation.
2 CORINTHIANS 5:19

"I, even, I, am he who blots out
  your transgressions, for my own sake,
  and remembers your sins no more," says the
  LORD.
ISAIAH 43:25

Blessed is he
  whose transgressions are forgiven,
  whose sins are covered.
Blessed is the man
  whose sin the LORD does not count against him
  and in whose spirit is no deceit.
PSALM 32:1–2

Peter came to Jesus and asked, "Lord, how many times shall I forgive my brother when he sins against me? Up to seven times?" Jesus answered, "I tell you, not seven times, but seventy-seven times."

MATTHEW 18:21–22

In Christ we have redemption through his blood, the forgiveness of sins, in accordance with the riches of God's grace that he lavished on us with all wisdom and understanding.

EPHESIANS 1:7–8

God has rescued us from the dominion of darkness and brought us into the kingdom of the Son he loves, in whom we have redemption, the forgiveness of sins.

COLOSSIANS 1:13–14

You are forgiving and good, O Lord,
    abounding in love to all who call to you.

PSALM 86:5

The blood of Jesus, God's Son, purifies us from all sin. If we claim to be without sin, we deceive ourselves and the truth is not in us. If we confess our sins, God is faithful and just and will forgive us our sins and purify us from all unrighteousness.

1 JOHN 1:7–9

The LORD is slow to anger, abounding in love and forgiving sin and rebellion.
NUMBERS 14:18

Forgive us our debts, as we also have forgiven our debtors. And lead us not into temptation, but deliver us from the evil one.
MATTHEW 6:12–13

When we were overwhelmed by sins,
    you forgave our transgressions, O LORD.
PSALM 65:3

Jesus said, "If you forgive men when they sin against you, your heavenly Father will also forgive you. But if you do not forgive men their sins, your Father will not forgive your sins."
MATTHEW 6:14–15

In Christ God forgave you.
EPHESIANS 4:32

"If my people, who are called by my name, will humble themselves and pray and seek my face and turn from their wicked ways, then will I hear from heaven and will forgive their sin and will heal their land," says the LORD.
2 CHRONICLES 7:14

FORGIVENESS

You are a forgiving God, gracious and compassionate, slow to anger and abounding in love.

NEHEMIAH 9:17

If anyone has caused grief ... the punishment inflicted on him by the majority is sufficient for him. Now instead, you ought to forgive and comfort him, so that he will not be overwhelmed by excessive sorrow. I urge you, therefore, to reaffirm your love for him.

2 CORINTHIANS 2:5–8

God was pleased to have all his fullness dwell in Christ, and through him to reconcile to himself all things, whether things on earth or things in heaven, by making peace through his blood, shed on the cross.

COLOSSIANS 1:19–20

When we've been wronged, it's pretty tough to muster up feelings of love for the one who's offended us. When our child arrives home for dinner two hours late, loving words aren't usually on our list of immediate responses. When our husband inserts his foot into his mouth at a party and insults us, it usually isn't love he sees reflected on our face.

While defense may be one way to handle hurt, a method that promises more healing is forgiveness. Here's how:

- *Put love on the list of alternatives for dealing with hurt.* Love won't naturally flow out of offense. We have to be intentional about choosing love.

- *Look at people in parts.* Try to isolate the incident and the action from the person who committed it. Look past the act to see that person's needs.

- *Remember how much we've needed forgiveness.* A review of our own errors may make those of another not look so bad.

Paul asked Philemon not just to take runaway slave Onesimus back but to love him as a part of his own family. While it may not be the most natural response after an offense, love is the most healing.

Two are better than one,
>   because they have a good return for their work:
If one falls down,
>   his friend can help him up.
But pity the man who falls
>   and has no one to help him up!
Also, if two lie down together, they will keep warm.
>   But how can one keep warm alone?
Though one may be overpowered,
>   two can defend themselves.
A cord of three strands is not quickly broken.

ECCLESIASTES 4:9–12

A man of many companions may come to ruin,
>   but there is a friend who sticks closer than a
>   brother.

PROVERBS 18:24

Wounds from a friend can be trusted.

PROVERBS 27:6

Perfume and incense bring joy to the heart,
>   and the pleasantness of one's friend springs from his
>   earnest counsel.

PROVERBS 27:9

Be devoted to one another in brotherly love. Honor one another above yourselves.

ROMANS 12:10

If we walk in the light, as Christ is in the light, we have fellowship with one another.

1 JOHN 1:7

A despairing man should have the devotion of his
friends.

JOB 6:14

Jesus said, "Greater love has no one than this, that he lay down his life for his friends. You are my friends if you do what I command. I no longer call you servants, because a servant does not know his master's business. Instead, I have called you friends."

JOHN 15:13–15

A friend loves at all times,
and a brother is born for adversity.

PROVERBS 17:17

My intercessor is my friend
as my eyes pour out tears to God.

JOB 16:20

Let no debt remain outstanding, except the continuing debt to love one another.

ROMANS 13:8

Be perfectly united in mind and thought.

1 CORINTHIANS 1:10

He who loves a pure heart and whose speech is
    gracious
    will have the king for his friend.

PROVERBS 22:11

Ruth told Naomi, "Where you go I will go, and where you stay I will stay. Your people will be my people and your God my God. Where you die I will die, and there I will be buried. May the LORD deal with me, be it ever so severely, if anything but death separates you and me."

RUTH 1:16–17

A toadstool can pop up overnight. An oak tree, on the
other hand, takes years to mature to full size. Let's take a
look at the friendships in our lives. Have they popped
up like toadstools or have they matured as oaks?

Intimacy—genuine intimacy—is not immediate. We
expect it to be. The world around us tells us it is. Singles
walk into bars and come out as couples. Acquaintances
share statistics about kids' ages and skills and assume
they've connected.

Toadstool friendships don't require much investment.
We camp on common ground, enjoy the instant intimacy that arises and then when it's gone, move on to
another spot. But oak tree friends grow only with a
greater investment. Time, availability, vulnerability, risk,
spontaneity—these are the ingredients that fertilize an
oak tree friendship.

Are we growing toadstool or oak tree friendships? We'll
probably want some of each. But we'll only get the last-
ing value of an oak tree friendship if we're willing to
invest ourselves in our friends.

GOSSIP

Without wood a fire goes out;
  without gossip a quarrel dies down.

PROVERBS 26:20

May the words of my mouth
  and the meditation of my heart
  be pleasing in your sight,
  O LORD, my Rock and my Redeemer.

PSALM 19:14

A gossip separates close friends.

PROVERBS 16:28

Reckless words pierce like a sword,
  but the tongue of the wise brings healing.

PROVERBS 12:18

A gossip betrays a confidence;
  so avoid a man who talks too much.

PROVERBS 20:19

A trustworthy man keeps a secret.

PROVERBS 11:13

*Do not let any unwholesome talk come out of your
mouths.*

EPHESIANS 4:29

GOSSIP

Do to others what you would have them do to you.
MATTHEW 7:12

He who covers over an offense promotes love,
> but whoever repeats the matter separates close
> friends.

PROVERBS 17:9

Truthful lips endure forever,
> but a lying tongue lasts only a moment.

There is deceit in the hearts of those who plot evil,
> but joy for those who promote peace.

No harm befalls the righteous,
> but the wicked have their fill of trouble.

The LORD detests lying lips,
> but he delights in men who are truthful.

PROVERBS 12:19–22

He who guards his mouth and his tongue
> keeps himself from calamity.

PROVERBS 21:23

When words are many, sin is not absent,
> but he who holds his tongue is wise.

PROVERBS 10:19

The tongue that brings healing is a tree of life.

PROVERBS 15:4

Show proper respect to everyone: Love the brotherhood of believers.

1 PETER 2:17

If anyone speaks, he should do it as one speaking the very words of God

1 PETER 4:11

DEVOTIONAL THOUGHT
ON GOSSIP

The tongue is often the most out-of-shape muscle in the human body. While aerobics and jogging are good for body and soul, a lifelong practice of exercise for the tongue will get that muscle in shape too.

Begin by tabulating your present rate of tongue slips. You know, those cruel or sarcastic remarks aimed at tearing down rather than building up. Still unclear? Well, put it this way: A slip of the tongue is anything you wouldn't say in the presence of Jesus.

One to two slips per hour of conversation? You're in pretty good shape, although you could still benefit from daily workouts. Make it a practice to think before you speak and then ask forgiveness for your blunders.

Four to eight slips per hour? Oooh. You need to check the attitudes of your heart. Greedy? Critical? Impatient? Probably. A session of heart-cleansing confession may be helpful.

More than eight slips an hour? Ahhh. This is cause for alarm. You need daily attendance in an exercise program for the prayer and support needed to alter your habit.

Obtain a lifetime membership in an exercise program for the tongue. You'll be better off for it and so will those around you.

GRANDPARENTS

The righteous will flourish like a palm tree,
    they will grow like a cedar of Lebanon;
planted in the house of the LORD,
    they will flourish in the courts of our God.
They will still bear fruit in old age,
    they will stay fresh and green.

PSALM 92:12–14

May you live to see your children's children.

PSALM 128:6

Children's children are a crown to the aged,
    and parents are the pride of their children.

PROVERBS 17:6

From everlasting to everlasting
    the LORD'S love is with those who fear him,
    and his righteousness with
    their children's children—
with those who keep his covenant
    and remember to obey his precepts.

PSALM 103:17–18

Gray hair is a crown of splendor;
    it is attained by a righteous life.

PROVERBS 16:31

He who fears the LORD has a secure fortress,
    and for his children it will be a refuge.
PROVERBS 14:26

"Even to your old age and gray hairs
    I am he," says the LORD,
    "I am he who will sustain you.
I have made you and I will carry you;
    I will sustain you and I will rescue you."
ISAIAH 46:4

Is not wisdom found among the aged?
    Does not long life bring understanding?
JOB 12:12

I will open my mouth in parables,
    I will utter hidden things, things from of old—
what we have heard and known,
    what our fathers have told us.
We will not hide them from their children;
    we will tell the next generation
the praiseworthy deeds of the LORD,
    his power, and the wonders he has done.
PSALM 78:2–4

The glory of young men is their strength,
gray hair the splendor of the old.

PROVERBS 20:29

Even when I am old and gray,
do not forsake me, O God,
till I declare your power to the next generation,
your might to all who are to come.

PSALM 71:18

*[Older women] can train the younger women to love
their husbands and children.*

TITUS 2:4

Laps open and ready for watching post-nap cartoons.
Eyes crinkling in response to cartwheels and somersaults
across the backyard. Heads thrown back in laughter during tickle sessions. Checks hidden in birthday cards.
Games played on tables still sticky from holiday baking.
Walks, hand in hand, through the leaves in the park. Ice
cream on cones, stacked scoop upon scoop, licked in
unison on an outside bench. Wrinkly hands curled atop
piano keys while others gather around to listen.

Grandparents. All bring an offering that can be dupli-
cated by no other. An offering of wisdom that comes
from living a lifetime. An offering of patience hewn out
of trial. An offering of laughter that has been learned
through making the most out of both prosperous and
lean times.

Indeed, they "still bear fruit in old age." They "stay
fresh and green."

GUIDANCE

The LORD will guide you always
    he will satisfy your needs in a sun-scorched land
    and will strengthen your frame.
You will be like a well-watered garden,
    like a spring whose waters never fail.

ISAIAH 58:11

This God is our God for ever and ever;
    he will be our guide even to the end.

PSALM 48:14

Trust in the LORD with all your heart
    and lean not on your own understanding;
in all your ways acknowledge him,
    and he will make your paths straight.

PROVERBS 3:5–6

This is what the LORD says—
    your Redeemer, the Holy One of Israel:
"I am the LORD your God,
    who teaches you what is best for you,
    who directs you in the way you should go."

ISAIAH 48:17

Keep your father's commands
    and do not forsake your mother's teaching.

Bind them upon your heart forever;
>   fasten them around your neck.
When you walk, they will guide you;
>   when you sleep, they will watch over you;
>   when you awake, they will speak to you.
For these commands are a lamp,
>   this teaching is a light,
and the corrections of discipline
>   are the way to life.

PROVERBS 6:20–23

Since you are my rock and my fortress, O LORD,
>   for the sake of your name lead and guide me.

PSALM 31:3

If any of you lacks wisdom, he should ask God, who gives generously to all without finding fault, and it will be given to him.

JAMES 1:5

Commit to the LORD whatever you do,
>   and your plans will succeed.

PROVERBS 16:3

"I know the plans I have for you," declares the LORD, "plans to prosper you and not to harm you, plans to give

you hope and a future."
JEREMIAH 29:11

The LORD guards the course of the just
and protects the way of his faithful ones.

PROVERBS 2:8

Show me your ways, O LORD,
teach me your paths;
guide me in your truth and teach me,
for you are God my Savior,
and my hope is in you all day long.

PSALM 25:4–5

*Jesus said, "When he, the Spirit of truth, comes, he will
guide you into all truth. He will not speak on his own;
he will speak only what he hears, and he will tell you
what is yet to come."*

JOHN 16:13

"I will instruct you and teach you in the way you
should go;
I will counsel you and watch over you," says the
LORD.

PSALM 32:8

GUIDANCE

In your unfailing love you will
     lead the people you have redeemed, O LORD.
In your strength you will guide them
     to your holy dwelling.

EXODUS 15:13

Search me, O God, and know my heart;
     test me and know my anxious thoughts.
See if there is any offensive way in me,
     and lead me in the way everlasting.

PSALM 139:23–24

*Whether you turn to the right or to the left, your ears
will hear a voice behind you, saying, "This is the way;
walk in it."*

ISAIAH 30:21

"I guide you in the way of wisdom
     and lead you along straight paths.
When you walk, your steps will not be hampered;
     when you run, you will not stumble," says the
LORD.

PROVERBS 4:11–12

The way of a fool seems right to him,
     but a wise man listens to advice.

PROVERBS 12:15

GUIDANCE

Let us go up to the mountain of the LORD,
    to the house of the God of Jacob.
He will teach us his ways,
    so that we may walk in his paths.

ISAIAH 2:3

This is what the LORD says:
"Stand at the crossroads and look;
    ask for the ancient paths,
ask where the good way is, and walk in it,
    and you will find rest for your souls."

JEREMIAH 6:16

Teach me to do your will,
    for you are my God;
may your good Spirit
    lead me on level ground.

PSALM 143:10

God allows us—his children—to lay our burdens and cares on him. In such times I suggest a prayer with four petitions:

1. Dear Lord, show me what resources I have.
2. What are my alternatives in this situation?
3. Guide me to the best option. Show me why I should choose it.
4. I trust you to show me what to do next.
   Thank you for your never-failing kindness.

Life involves a series of choices. Because decision-making is such a routine part of life, I sometimes forget that every course of action I select affects some young imitator. I find that I often live by trial and error, and I need to learn instead to live by trusting God. Skillful living starts with hearing—and obeying—God's commands.

A cheerful look brings joy to the heart,
    and good news gives health to the bones.

PROVERBS 15:30

*Food does not bring us near to God; we are no worse if
we do not eat, and no better if we do. Be careful, however,
that the exercise of your freedom does not become a
stumbling block.*

1 CORINTHIANS 8:8–9

*The kingdom of God is not a matter of eating and
drinking, but of righteousness, peace and joy in the
Holy Spirit.*

ROMANS 14:17

*Train yourself to be godly. For physical training is of
some value, but godliness has value for all things, holding
promise for both the present life and the life to
come.*

1 TIMOTHY 4:7–8

*Anyone who lives on milk, being still an infant, is not
acquainted with the teaching about righteousness. But
solid food is for the mature, who by constant use have
trained themselves to distinguish good from evil.*

HEBREWS 5:13–14

*Say "No" to ungodliness and worldly passions, and ...
live self-controlled, upright and godly lives in this present age.*
TITUS 2:12

*I press on toward the goal to win the prize for which
God has called me heavenward in Christ Jesus.*
PHILIPPIANS 3:14

*Since we are surrounded by such a great cloud of witnesses, let us throw off everything that hinders and the
sin that so easily entangles, and let us run with perseverance the race marked out for us. Let us fix our eyes
on Jesus, the author and perfecter of our faith.*
HEBREWS 12:1–2

Long life to you! Good health to you and your household! And good health to all that is yours!
1 SAMUEL 25:6

Trust in the LORD with all your heart
    and lean not on your own understanding;
in all your ways acknowledge him,
    and he will make your paths straight.
Do not be wise in your own eyes;
    fear the LORD and shun evil.

This will bring health to your body
and nourishment to your bones.

PROVERBS 3:5–8

Above all else, guard your heart,
for it is the wellspring of life.

PROVERBS 4:23

*Do you not know that your body is a temple of the Holy
Spirit, who is in you, whom you have received from God?
You are not your own; you were bought at a price. There-
fore honor God with your body.*

1 CORINTHIANS 6:19–20

Wisdom is a tree of life to those who embrace her;
those who lay hold of her will be blessed.

PROVERBS 3:18

*May God himself, the God of peace, sanctify you through
and through. May your whole spirit, soul and body be
kept blameless at the coming of our Lord Jesus Christ.*

1 THESSALONIANS 5:23

A heart at peace gives life to the body.

PROVERBS 14:30

DEVOTIONAL THOUGHT
ON HEALTHY LIVING

Experts knowingly tout the benefits of physical fitness on general well-being. Bottom line, when we're out of shape, we don't feel good and we tire easily.

The break many moms need is simply a walk around the block to feel the fresh air and get the blood flowing. Some mothers need better nutrition—something other than leftover peanut-butter-and-jelly sandwiches and dry cereal. And others need to lie down for a half-hour nap.

While it's sometimes next to impossible to get that needed break, we can learn to take advantage of odd moments here and there. We can get up early and go for a jog while our husband is home. We can trade kids with a friend and take a walk in the neighborhood. Weekends are a great time to begin a habit and carry it on into the next week.

For many of us with overcrowded schedules, physical fitness is one of the first things to go. We figure no one will notice. Wrong. Whether or not the lack of love for our bodies shows on the outside, the inside suffers. And eventually, the damage will be demonstrated in the form of impatience, irritability and general grouchiness. If a woman doesn't feel good about herself, she's less likely to treat others with goodness.

The King will say, "I was hungry and you gave me something to eat, I was thirsty and you gave me something to drink, I was a stranger and you invited me in, I needed clothes and you clothed me, I was sick and you looked after me, I was in prison and you came to visit me." Then the righteous will answer him, "Lord, when did we see you hungry and feed you, or thirsty and give you something to drink? When did we see you a stranger and invite you in, or needing clothes and clothe you? When did we see you sick or in prison and go to visit you?" The King will reply, "I tell you the truth, whatever you did for one of the least of these brothers of mine, you did for me."

MATTHEW 25:34–40

Share with God's people who are in need. Practice hospitality.

ROMANS 12:13

"Is not this the kind of fasting I have chosen:
to loose the chains of injustice
    and untie the cords of the yoke,
to set the oppressed free
    and break every yoke?
Is it not to share your food with the hungry

and to provide the poor wanderer with shelter—
when you see the naked, to clothe him,
and not to turn away from your own flesh and
blood?
Then your light will break forth like the dawn,
and your healing will quickly appear;
then your righteousness will go before you,
and the glory of the LORD will be your rear
guard," declares the LORD.

ISAIAH 58:6–8

*Then Jesus said to his host, "When you give a luncheon
or dinner, do not invite your friends, your brothers or
relatives, or your rich neighbors; if you do, they may
invite you back and so you will be repaid. But when
you give a banquet, invite the poor, the crippled, the
lame, the blind, and you will be blessed. Although they
cannot repay you, you will be repaid at the resurrection
of the righteous."*

LUKE 14:12–14

*Be hospitable, one who loves what is good, who is self-
controlled, upright, holy and disciplined.*

TITUS 1:8

HOSPITALITY

Do not forget to entertain strangers, for by so doing some people have entertained angels without knowing it.

HEBREWS 13:2

Abraham looked up and saw three men standing nearby. When he saw them, he hurried from the entrance of his tent to meet them and bowed low to the ground. He said, "If I have found favor in your eyes, my lord, do not pass your servant by. Let a little water be brought, and then you may all wash your feet and rest under this tree. Let me get you something to eat, so you can be refreshed and then go on your way—now that you have come to your servant." "Very well," they answered, "do as you say."

GENESIS 18:2–5

Offer hospitality to one another without grumbling. … If anyone serves, he should do it with the strength God provides, so that in all things God may be praised through Jesus Christ.

1 PETER 4:9, 11

Do not forget to do good and to share with others, for with such sacrifices God is pleased.

HEBREWS 13:16

DEVOTIONAL THOUGHT ON HOSPITALITY

We haven't finished painting yet. We don't have enough chairs. We don't know what to say to people. Nevertheless, we have everything we need to become hospitable.

We tend to view hospitality as a kind of pass/fail performance. When someone invites us over, we feel compelled to reciprocate—but do it better. But rather than an elaborate show of pretty possessions, fancy food or talented talk, true hospitality is simply sharing ourselves and what is ours with someone else. Our home. Our family. Our personality. Our sagging couch and mismatched dishes. Our hand-made tablecloth passed down from our grandmother. Our cans of soup and our cherished stories of our own traditions.

After all, folks are most comfortable in a place where they can feel at home. Better a happy guest who notices our dust and chipped dishes but feels truly welcome than a guest who heaps praise on our beautiful home but inside only feels inadequate in comparison.

Let's keep it simple. True hospitality is sharing ourselves and what is ours with another.

JOY

May the God of hope fill you with all joy and peace as you trust in him, so that you may overflow with hope by the power of the Holy Spirit.

ROMANS 15:13

Light is shed upon the righteous
and joy on the upright in heart.

PSALM 97:11

God will yet fill your mouth with laughter
and your lips with shouts of joy.

JOB 8:21

God's favor lasts a lifetime;
weeping may remain for a night,
but rejoicing comes in the morning.

PSALM 30:5

Rejoice in the LORD and be glad, you righteous;
sing, all you who are upright in heart!

PSALM 32:11

O LORD, may all who seek you
rejoice and be glad in you;

JOY

may those who love your salvation always say,
"Let God be exalted!"

PSALM 70:4

The ransomed of the LORD will return.
They will enter Zion with singing;
everlasting joy will crown their heads.
Gladness and joy will overtake them,
and sorrow and sighing will flee away.

ISAIAH 51:11

Let all who take refuge in you be glad, O LORD;
let them ever sing for joy.
Spread your protection over them,
that those who love your name may rejoice in
you.

PSALM 5:11

Shout for joy to the LORD, all the earth.
Worship the LORD with gladness;
come before him with joyful songs.

PSALM 100:1–2

O LORD, I rejoice in following your statutes
as one rejoices in great riches.

PSALM 119:14

JOY

Those who sow in tears
will reap with songs of joy.
PSALM 126:5

The prospect of the righteous is joy.
PROVERBS 10:28

You will go out in joy
and be led forth in peace;
the mountains and hills
will burst into song before you,
and all the trees of the field
will clap their hands.
ISAIAH 55:12

Rejoice in the LORD your God,
for he has given you
the autumn rains in righteousness.
He sends you abundant showers,
both autumn and spring rains, as before.
JOEL 2:23

Jesus said, "Until now you have not asked for anything in my name. Ask and you will receive, and your joy will be complete."
JOHN 16:24

GOD'S WORDS OF LIFE ON

JOY

*Consider it pure joy ... whenever you face trials of
many kinds, because you know that the testing of your
faith develops perseverance.*
JAMES 1:2–3

*The kingdom of God is ... righteousness, peace and joy
in the Holy Spirit.*
ROMANS 14:17

Rejoice in the Lord always. I will say it again: Rejoice!
PHILIPPIANS 4:4

The joy of the LORD is your strength.
NEHEMIAH 8:10

The LORD has done great things for us,
    and we are filled with joy.
PSALM 126:3

*Blessed are you when men hate you, when they exclude
you and insult you and reject your name as evil, because
of the Son of Man. Rejoice in that day and leap for joy,
because great is your reward in heaven. For that is how
their fathers treated the prophets.*
LUKE 6:22–23

You have made known to me the path of life;
    O LORD,
        you will fill me with joy in your presence,
        with eternal pleasures at your right hand.

PSALM 16:11

The precepts of the LORD are right,
    giving joy to the heart.
The commands of the LORD are radiant,
    giving light to the eyes.

PSALM 19:8

Your statutes, LORD, are my heritage forever;
    they are the joy of my heart.

PSALM 119:111

We wait in hope for the LORD;
    he is our help and our shield.
In him our hearts rejoice,
    for we trust in his holy name.

PSALM 33:20–21

I delight greatly in the LORD;
    my soul rejoices in my God.

For he has clothed me with garments of salvation.

ISAIAH 61:10

Hannah prayed and said, "My heart rejoices in the LORD; in the LORD my horn is lifted high."

1 SAMUEL 2:1

Mary said, "My soul glorifies the Lord and my spirit rejoices in God my Savior."

LUKE 1:46–47

You believe in Christ and are filled with an inexpressible and glorious joy.

1 PETER 1:8

Let us rejoice and be glad and give God glory! For the wedding of the Lamb has come, and his bride has made herself ready.

REVELATION 19:7

Rejoice that you participate in the sufferings of Christ, so that you may be overjoyed when his glory is revealed.

1 PETER 4:13

JOY

You are to rejoice before the LORD your God in everything you put your hand to.

DEUTERONOMY 12:18

To him who is able to keep you from falling and to present you before his glorious presence without fault and with great joy—to the only God our Savior be glory, majesty, power and authority, through Jesus Christ our Lord, before all ages, now and forevermore!

JUDE 24–25

I have no greater joy than to hear that my children are walking in the truth.

3 JOHN 4

DEVOTIONAL THOUGHT
ON JOY

The philosopher Friedrich Nietzsche once criticized Christians by saying, "I would believe in their salvation if they looked a little more like people who have been saved."

Joy is more than happiness. The word happiness comes from the root hap which means "chance." Where happiness is circumstantial, joy is not. Joy is an unshakable confidence in the truths of God, despite circumstances. When our children see an unshakable confidence in the life of one who knows God personally, they are impressed and drawn to know him themselves.

If we want folks like Nietzsche (and our children) to believe in our God, we'll need more than a pasted-on smile of chance happiness. We'll need joy.

Dear Lord, please give me a reason to taste the true joy of being confident in you. Show me the difference between the chance happiness of our world and the unshakable confidence of knowing your character to be unchanging and true. May this fruit of confidence be evidenced in my outlook, my attitudes, my bearing, and my being, that I might attract others to your truth.

Amen.

KINDNESS

Love is kind. It does not envy, it does not boast, it is not proud.

1 CORINTHIANS 13:4

Carry each other's burdens, and in this way you will fulfill the law of Christ.

GALATIANS 6:2

As we have opportunity, let us do good to all people.

GALATIANS 6:10

As God's chosen people, holy and dearly loved, clothe yourselves with compassion, kindness, humility, gentleness and patience.

COLOSSIANS 3:12

Make every effort to add to your faith ... brotherly kindness; and to brotherly kindness, love. For if you possess these qualities in increasing measure, they will keep you from being ineffective and unproductive in your knowledge of our Lord Jesus Christ.

2 PETER 1:5, 7–8

If anyone has material possessions and sees his brother in need but has no pity on him, how can the love of

God be in him? Dear children, let us not love with words or tongue but with actions and in truth.
1 JOHN 3:17–18

Ruth bowed down with her face to the ground. She exclaimed, "Why have I found such favor in your eyes that you notice me—a foreigner?" Boaz replied, "I've been told all about what you have done for your mother-in-law since the death of your husband—how you left your father and mother and your homeland and came to live with a people you did not know before. May the LORD repay you for what you have done. May you be richly rewarded by the LORD, the God of Israel, under whose wings you have come to take refuge."
RUTH 2:10–12

The fruit of the Spirit is love, joy, peace, patience, kindness, goodness, faithfulness.
GALATIANS 5:22

When the kindness and love of God our Savior appeared, he saved us, not because of righteous things we had done, but because of his mercy.
TITUS 3:4–5

Jesus said, "If anyone gives even a cup of cold water to one of these little ones because he is my disciple, I tell you the truth, he will certainly not lose his reward."
MATTHEW 10:42

Be kind and compassionate to one another, forgiving each other, just as in Christ God forgave you.
EPHESIANS 4:32

Jesus said, "In everything, do to others what you would have them do to you, for this sums up the Law and the Prophets."
MATTHEW 7:12

DEVOTIONAL THOUGHT
on KINDNESS

A little girl was overheard praying, "Lord, make all the bad people good and all the good people nice." God wants his people to be good. But goodness isn't enough.

In addition to being good, we need to be kind. Planted by the God who is wholly good, the quality of goodness takes root within our hearts, growing all around and through our beliefs and motivations. Our kindness is then the fruitful expression on the outside of the goodness that has been cultivated within.

Goodness recognizes a need. Kindness meets it. Goodness stands against hunger. Kindness sends money to the poor to buy food. Goodness knows that we are to care for the needy. Kindness goes to the hospital with an unwed mother and coaches her through labor and delivery. Goodness realizes there's a job to be done. Kindness does the job.

Dear Lord, please teach me to demonstrate goodness by being kind. Move me past the sidelines of concern to the arena of action. As you work in my life to make me good—more like you—please make me nice as well.

Amen.

GOD'S WORDS OF LIFE ON
LISTENING

In the morning, O LORD, you hear my voice;
in the morning I lay my requests before you
and wait in expectation.

PSALM 5:3

"Listen, listen to me, and eat what is good
and your soul will delight in the richest of fare.
Give ear and come to me;
hear me, that your soul may live," declares the
LORD.

ISAIAH 55:2–3

Wisdom calls, "Whoever listens to me will live in
safety
and be at ease, without fear of harm."

PROVERBS 1:20, 33

Pay attention to my wisdom,
listen well to my words of insight,
that you may maintain discretion
and your lips may preserve knowledge.

PROVERBS 5:1–2

*Jesus said, "My sheep listen to my voice; I know them,
and they follow me."*

JOHN 10:27

LISTENING

The Holy Spirit says, "Today, if you hear God's voice, do not harden your hearts."

HEBREWS 3:7-8

He who listens to a life-giving rebuke
   will be at home among the wise.

PROVERBS 15:31

Jesus said, "Everyone who listens to the Father and learns from him comes to me."

JOHN 6:45

John wrote, "We are from God, and whoever knows God listens to us; but whoever is not from God does not listen to us. This is how we recognize the Spirit of truth and the spirit of falsehood."

1 JOHN 4:6

Anyone who listens to the word but does not do what it says is like a man who looks at his face in a mirror and, after looking at himself, goes away and immediately forgets what he looks like.

JAMES 1:23-24

Jesus said, "Here I am! I stand at the door and knock. If anyone hears my voice and opens the door, I will

---

come in and eat with him, and he with me."
REVELATION 3:20

The LORD said, "Go out and stand on the mountain in the presence of the LORD, for the LORD is about to pass by." Then a great and powerful wind tore the mountains apart and shattered the rocks before the LORD, but the LORD was not in the wind. After the wind there was an earthquake, but the LORD was not in the earthquake. After the earthquake came a fire, but the LORD was not in the fire. And after the fire came a gentle whisper. When Elijah heard it, he pulled his cloak over his face and went out and stood at the mouth of the cave.
1 KINGS 19:11–13

Jesus said, "The man who enters by the gate is the shepherd of his sheep. The watchman opens the gate for him, and the sheep listen to his voice. He calls his own sheep by name and leads them out. When he has brought out all his own, he goes on ahead of them, and his sheep follow him because they know his voice."
JOHN 10:2–4

DEVOTIONAL THOUGHT ON LISTENING

God has something to say to you. Each new day brings a lesson from his lips. Are you listening?

Notice how 1 Samuel 3 begins: "In those days the word of the LORD was rare; there were not many visions." Sounds like today, doesn't it? God seems so silent in our world! Rarely do we seem to hear his voice.

But all that changed in Israel's day because a boy was willing to listen. Samuel heard God call him in the night and responded in obedience. God's message was hard. Samuel had to deliver a tough tale of judgment to Eli, the priest and his superior. But Samuel followed through on God's word.

Truly, one person can make a difference! One woman. One mother. One child.

When you lay your head down to sleep and when your feet hit the floor again, prick up your ears for the voice of God. God's word may be rare to those who are deaf, but to those who are listening, he speaks.

LONELINESS

The LORD your God goes with you; he will never leave you nor forsake you.

DEUTERONOMY 31:6

I am always with you; LORD,
 you hold me by my right hand.

PSALM 73:23

Jesus said, "Surely I am with you always, to the very end of the age."

MATTHEW 28:20

Jesus said, "I will not leave you as orphans; I will come to you."

JOHN 14:18

In Christ we who are many form one body, and each member belongs to all the others.

ROMANS 12:5

You are with me; LORD,
your rod and your staff,
 they comfort me.

PSALM 23:4

LONELINESS

God sets the lonely in families.

PSALM 68:6

Paul wrote, "At my first defense, no one came to my support, but everyone deserted me. May it not be held against them. But the Lord stood at my side and gave me strength."

2 TIMOTHY 4:16–17

God said, "I am with you and will watch over you wherever you go. ... I will not leave you until I have done what I have promised you."

GENESIS 28:15

Those who know your name will trust in you,
     for you, LORD, have never forsaken
those who seek you.

PSALM 9:10

God has said, "Never will I leave you; never will I forsake you."

HEBREWS 13:5

Jesus said, "Do not let your hearts be troubled. Trust in God; trust also in me."

JOHN 14:1

The LORD builds up Jerusalem;
    he gathers the exiles of Israel.
He heals the brokenhearted
    and binds up their wounds.

PSALM 147:2–3

Turn to me and be gracious to me, O LORD,
    for I am lonely and afflicted.
The troubles of my heart have multiplied;
    free me from my anguish.

PSALM 25:16–17

Though my father and mother forsake me,
    the LORD will receive me.

PSALM 27:10

"Though the mountains be shaken
    and the hills be removed,
yet my unfailing love for you will not be shaken
    nor my covenant of peace be removed,"
    says the LORD, who has compassion on you.

ISAIAH 54:10

*The LORD God said, "It is not good for the man to be
alone. I will make a helper suitable for him."*
GENESIS 2:18

My soul finds rest in God alone;
  my salvation comes from him.
He alone is my rock and my salvation;
  he is my fortress, I will never be shaken.

PSALM 62:1–2

The LORD lifted the needy out of their affliction
  and increased their families like flocks.
The upright see and rejoice. ...
  Whoever is wise, let him heed these things
and consider the great love of the LORD.

PSALM 107:41–43

The ransomed of the LORD will return.
  They will enter Zion with singing;
everlasting joy will crown their heads.
  Gladness and joy will overtake them,
and sorrow and sighing will flee away.

ISAIAH 51:11

The LORD is near to all who call on him,
  to all who call on him in truth.

PSALM 145:18

"My Presence goes with you," says the LORD, "and I will give you rest."

EXODUS 33:14

Now the dwelling of God is with men, and he will live with them. They will be his people, and God himself will be with them and be their God. He will wipe every tear from their eyes.

REVELATION 21:3–4

Devotional Thought
on Loneliness

All of us have struggled at some point with loneliness and the need for friendship. In such a spot, we often wonder how to reach out and make the friends we need.

If you want to make a friend, creating a clique may be the smartest move you can make. Those who are serious about friend-making start small.

Technically, a clique is defined as a narrow and exclusive group of people who hold the same interests, views and beliefs. Leaving the narrow and exclusive behind, pick out the healthy ingredients of cliques and with them form the foundation of a friendship. Start small by selecting a few folks who share your interests, views and purposes for life.

Solomon seemed to understand the wisdom of selective friendship. Writing in Proverbs 18:24 he says, "A man of many companions may come to ruin, but there is a friend who sticks closer than a brother." There is wisdom in starting small in friend-making. Once you've got the technique down, you may be ready to reach out more boldly. But to begin with, create a clique.

LOVE

How great is the love the Father has lavished on us, that we should be called children of God! And that is what we are!
1 JOHN 3:1

Jesus said, "Love each other as I have loved you."
JOHN 15:12

Be devoted to one another in brotherly love. Honor one another above yourselves.
ROMANS 12:10

Serve one another in love.
GALATIANS 5:13

How good and pleasant it is
    when brothers live together in unity!
PSALM 133:1

Live a life of love, just as Christ loved us and gave himself up for us as a fragrant offering and sacrifice to God.
EPHESIANS 5:2

May the Lord make your love increase and overflow for each other and for everyone else.
1 THESSALONIANS 3:12

LOVE

Live in harmony with one another; be sympathetic, love as brothers, be compassionate and humble.
1 PETER 3:8

As God's chosen people, holy and dearly loved, clothe yourselves with compassion, kindness, humility, gentleness and patience. … Over all these virtues put on love, which binds them all together in perfect unity.
COLOSSIANS 3:12, 14

Many waters cannot quench love;
    rivers cannot wash it away.
If one were to give
    all the wealth of his house for love,
    it would be utterly scorned.
SONG OF SONGS 8:7

Do everything in love.
1 CORINTHIANS 16:14

Let no debt remain outstanding, except the continuing debt to love one another.
ROMANS 13:8

Praise be to the LORD,
    for he showed his wonderful love to me.
PSALM 31:21

131

LOVE

How priceless is your unfailing love, O LORD!
Both high and low among men
   find refuge in the shadow of your wings.

PSALM 36:7

I will sing of the LORD'S great love forever;
   with my mouth I will make your faithfulness
known through all generations.

PSALM 89:1

*God demonstrates his own love for us in this: While we
were still sinners, Christ died for us.*

ROMANS 5:8

*I pray that you, being rooted and established in love,
may have power, together with all the saints, to grasp
how wide and long and high and deep is the love of
Christ.*

EPHESIANS 3:17–18

*Because of his great love for us, God, who is rich in
mercy, made us alive with Christ even when we were
dead in transgressions.*

EPHESIANS 2:4–5

LOVE

This is love: not that we loved God, but that he loved us and sent his Son as an atoning sacrifice for our sins.

1 JOHN 4:10

Love one another deeply, from the heart.

1 PETER 1:22

Let us love one another, for love comes from God. Everyone who loves has been born of God and knows God. Whoever does not love does not know God, because God is love.

1 JOHN 4:7–8

If I speak in the tongues of men and of angels, but have not love, I am only a resounding gong or a clanging cymbal. If I have the gift of prophecy and can fathom all mysteries and all knowledge, and if I have a faith that can move mountains, but have not love, I am nothing. If I give all I possess to the poor and surrender my body to the flames, but have not love, I gain nothing. Love is patient, love is kind. It does not envy, it does not boast, it is not proud. It is not rude, it is not self-seeking, it is not easily angered, it keeps no record of wrongs. Love does not delight in evil but rejoices with the truth. It always protects, always trusts, always hopes, always perseveres. Love never fails.

1 CORINTHIANS 13:1−8

The only thing that counts is faith expressing itself through love.

GALATIANS 5:6

No one has ever seen God; but if we love one another, God lives in us and his love is made complete in us.

1 JOHN 4:12

God so loved the world that he gave his one and only Son, that whoever believes in him shall not perish but have eternal life.

JOHN 3:16

This is how we know what love is: Jesus Christ laid down his life for us. And we ought to lay down our lives for our brothers.

1 JOHN 3:16

Love each other deeply, because love covers over a multitude of sins.

1 PETER 4:8

Without love, humans will die. It's that simple.

Decades ago, a cruel experiment was performed that underlines the most vital ingredients in healthy human development. In an orphanage, half the infants were cuddled and snuggled by the caretakers while the other half received only the most rudimentary attention through feedings and changings. In a few short weeks, the unattended, unloved, untouched babies began to show signs of failure to thrive. Without love, their lives waned.

Reaching into our world, God ministers to our need for love. In a revolutionary manner, God offers an unconditional love, filling to the brim our insatiable desire for personal acceptance.

Humans need love. God loves. He "so loved the world that he gave his one and only Son, that whoever believes in him shall not perish but have eternal life" (John 3:16). It's that simple.

Be still before the LORD and wait patiently for him;
   do not fret when men succeed in their ways,
   when they carry out their wicked schemes.

PSALM 37:7

Everyone should be quick to listen, slow to speak and slow to become angry.

JAMES 1:19

The end of a matter is better than its beginning,
   and patience is better than pride.

ECCLESIASTES 7:8

It is good to wait quietly
   for the salvation of the LORD.

LAMENTATIONS 3:26

Wait for the LORD;
   be strong and take heart
   and wait for the LORD.

PSALM 27:14

LORD, walking in the way of your laws,
   we wait for you;
your name and renown
   are the desire of our hearts.

ISAIAH 26:8

PATIENCE

Be joyful in hope, patient in affliction, faithful in prayer.

ROMANS 12:12

If we hope for what we do not yet have, we wait for it patiently.

ROMANS 8:25

I wait for the LORD, my soul waits,
    and in his word I put my hope.
My soul waits for the Lord
    more than watchmen wait for the morning.

PSALM 130:5–6

See how the farmer waits for the land to yield its valuable crop and how patient he is for the autumn and spring rains. You too, be patient and stand firm, because the Lord's coming is near.

JAMES 5:7–8

Love is patient.

1 CORINTHIANS 13:4

Be completely humble and gentle; be patient, bearing with one another in love.

EPHESIANS 4:2

PATIENCE

We pray this in order that you may live a life worthy of the Lord and may please him in every way: bearing fruit in every good work, growing in the knowledge of God, being strengthened with all power according to his glorious might so that you may have great endurance and patience.

COLOSSIANS 1:10–11

Be patient with everyone.

1 THESSALONIANS 5:14 .

You, O Lord, are a compassionate
    and gracious God,
slow to anger, abounding in love and faithfulness.

PSALM 86:15

The LORD longs to be gracious to you;
    he rises to show you compassion.
For the LORD is a God of justice.
    Blessed are all who wait for him!

ISAIAH 30:18

DEVOTIONAL THOUGHT
ON PATIENCE

We wait for everything. For the dryer to finish. For our husbands to get home. For the phone to ring. For the baby to wake. For the mail to come. For a car to pull up, returning our child safely home. For a job. For answers to prayer.

With so much experience, we're remarkably unskilled at waiting well. Waiting seems to us a colossal waste of time.

But the fact is that while we are waiting, God is working. To move us where he wants us to be. To readjust the lives of others so that his ultimate desires will be fulfilled. To bring about what will make us eventually Christlike, though not necessarily immediately comfortable.

What are you waiting for? And more to the point, how well are you waiting for it?

We must pray with a willingness to wait and wait with a willingness to pray. Waiting and praying go together. Like two shoes of a pair or two halves of a whole, they work as a team.

PEACE

Christ himself is our peace, who has made the two one and has destroyed the barrier, the dividing wall of hostility.

EPHESIANS 2:14

Let the peace of Christ rule in your hearts, since as members of one body you were called to peace.

COLOSSIANS 3:15

Do not be anxious about anything, but in everything, by prayer and petition, with thanksgiving, present your requests to God. And the peace of God, which transcends all understanding, will guard your hearts and your minds in Christ Jesus.

PHILIPPIANS 4:6–7

I will lie down and sleep in peace,
    for you alone, O LORD,
    make me dwell in safety.

PSALM 4:8

The LORD gives strength to his people;
    the LORD blesses his people with peace.

PSALM 29:11

PEACE

You, O Lord, will keep in perfect peace
    him whose mind is steadfast,
    because he trusts in you.

ISAIAH 26:3

The meek will inherit the land
    and enjoy great peace.

PSALM 37:11

Great peace have they who love your law, LORD,
    and nothing can make them stumble.

PSALM 119:165

When a man's ways are pleasing to the LORD,
    he makes even his enemies
    live at peace with him.

PROVERBS 16:7

To us a child is born,
    to us a son is given,
    and the government will be on his shoulders.
And he will be called
    Wonderful Counselor, Mighty God,
    Everlasting Father, Prince of Peace.

ISAIAH 9:6

PEACE

Christ came and preached peace to you who were far away and peace to those who were near. For through him we ... have access to the Father by one Spirit.
EPHESIANS 2:17–18

Grace and peace to you from God our Father and the Lord Jesus Christ.
PHILIPPIANS 1:2

"Peace, peace, to those far and near,"
  says the LORD. "And I will heal them."
ISAIAH 57:19

I will make a covenant of peace with them and rid the land of wild beasts so that they may live in the desert and sleep in the forests in safety. I will bless them and the places surrounding my hill. I will send down showers in season; there will be showers of blessing. The trees of the field will yield their fruit and the ground will yield its crops; the people will be secure in their land. They will know that I am the LORD.
EZEKIEL 34:25–27

The LORD bless you
  and keep you;

PEACE

the LORD make his face shine upon you
and be gracious to you;
the LORD turn his face toward you
and give you peace.

NUMBERS 6:24–26

Love and faithfulness meet together;
righteousness and peace kiss each other.

PSALM 85:10

*Make every effort to keep the unity of the Spirit through
the bond of peace.*

EPHESIANS 4:3

The God of peace will be with you.

PHILIPPIANS 4:9

*If it is possible, as far as it depends on you, live at peace
with everyone.*

ROMANS 12:18

*Peacemakers who sow in peace raise a harvest of right-
eousness.*

JAMES 3:18

PEACE

Jesus said, "Peace I leave with you; my peace I give you. I do not give to you as the world gives. Do not let your hearts be troubled and do not be afraid."

JOHN 14:27

Blessed are the peacemakers, for they will be called sons of God.

MATTHEW 5:9

Let us ... make very effort to do what leads to peace and to mutual edification.

ROMANS 14:19

Submit to God and be at peace with him;
    in this way prosperity will come to you.

JOB 22:21

DEVOTIONAL THOUGHT ON PEACE

A five-year-old tumbles into the kitchen from his adventures in backyard mud, bringing footprints of scum across a clean floor. The phone rings. The baby cries. The doorbell chimes. The dog barks. A harried mom grabs her temples in response to this torture.

Change scenes. The camera spans a spacious, private bath scene, circling around a tub filled to the brim with luxurious bubbles. A beautiful woman rests in the tub, hair pinned in loose curls, arms extended, eyes closed in an ecstasy of relaxation.

Supposedly, this second scene is a picture of peace. What I want to know is, where are the kids, what is the dog doing and who was at the door?

Contrary to the commercial, peace doesn't come in a package of bubble bath. It's not found in a tub or even behind a closed door. Peace comes when we fix our minds on God and on his stability in our chaotic days. No matter who is tromping a mess across our floors or standing impatiently at our doors, the unchangeable God is in charge of our days. Knowing *that* for a fact is peace.

PRAYER

"You will call upon me and come and pray to me, and I will listen to you," says the LORD. "You will seek me and find me when you seek me with all your heart."

JEREMIAH 29:12–13

"Before they call I will answer;
    while they are still speaking I will hear,"
        says the LORD.

ISAIAH 65:24

Jesus said, "Ask and it will be given to you; seek and you will find; knock and the door will be opened to you. For everyone who asks receives; he who seeks finds; and to him who knocks, the door will be opened."

MATTHEW 7:7–8

Jesus said, "I tell you that if two of you on earth agree about anything you ask for, it will be done for you by my Father in heaven. For where two or three come together in my name, there am I with them."

MATTHEW 18:19–20

Dear friends, if our hearts do not condemn us, we have confidence before God and receive from him anything we ask, because we obey his commands and do what pleases him.

1 JOHN 3:21–22

PRAYER

Jesus said, "When you pray, go into your room, close the door and pray to your Father, who is unseen. Then your Father, who sees what is done in secret, will reward you."
MATTHEW 6:6

The LORD is near to all who call on him,
    to all who call on him in truth.
PSALM 145:18

Jesus said, "If you believe, you will receive whatever you ask for in prayer."
MATTHEW 21:22

I call to God,
    and the LORD saves me.
Evening, morning and noon
    I cry out in distress,
    and he hears my voice.
PSALM 55:16–17

Pray continually.
1 THESSALONIANS 5:17

We have not stopped praying for you and asking God to fill you with the knowledge of his will through all spiritual wisdom and understanding.
COLOSSIANS 1:9

PRAYER

Pray in the Spirit on all occasions with all kinds of prayers and requests. With this in mind, be alert and always keep on praying for all the saints.

EPHESIANS 6:18

Let everyone who is godly pray to you, LORD,
    while you may be found;
surely when the mighty waters rise,
    they will not reach him.

PSALM 32:6

Hear, O LORD, my righteous plea;
    listen to my cry.
Give ear to my prayer—
    it does not rise from deceitful lips.

PSALM 17:1

Answer me when I call to you,
    O my righteous God.
Give me relief from my distress;
    be merciful to me and hear my prayer.

PSALM 4:1

The LORD has heard my cry for mercy;
    the LORD accepts my prayer.

PSALM 6:9

PRAYER

"Call to me and I will answer you and tell you great and unsearchable things you do not know," declares the LORD.

JEREMIAH 33:3

"He will call upon me, and I will answer him;
    I will be with him in trouble,
    I will deliver him and honor him,"
    declares the LORD.

PSALM 91:15

Let us ... approach the throne of grace with confidence, so that we may receive mercy and find grace to help us in our time of need.

HEBREWS 4:16

Jesus said, "I tell you the truth, my Father will give you whatever you ask in my name. Until now you have not asked for anything in my name. Ask and you will receive, and your joy will be complete."

JOHN 16:23–24

"If my people, who are called by my name, will humble themselves and pray and seek my face and turn from their wicked ways, then will I hear from heaven and *will forgive their sin and will heal their land," declares the LORD.*

2 CHRONICLES 7:14

I wait for you, O LORD;
　　you will answer, O Lord my God.

PSALM 38:15

If we confess our sins, God is faithful and just and will forgive us our sins and purify us from all unrighteousness.

1 JOHN 1:9

Very early in the morning, while it was still dark, Jesus got up, left the house and went off to a solitary place, where he prayed.

MARK 1:35

This is the confidence we have in approaching God: that if we ask anything according to his will, he hears us. And if we know that he hears us—whatever we ask—we know that we have what we asked of him.

1 JOHN 5:14–15

The eyes of the Lord are on the righteous and his ears are attentive to their prayer.

1 PETER 3:12

DEVOTIONAL THOUGHT
ON PRAYER

Can you think of any other exercise that yields more results than prayer?

We can converse with the God of the universe. When we bow our heads and utter God's name, we have an audience with a King more powerful than the leader of any earthly country.

- We're reminded that we're not alone. Even after a terrible tragedy or trial, God waits to be with us in prayer. Our trust is stretched.

- We're united to God and to other believers. When we pray for a sister, we're joined with her and with others who have the same desire. Our bond with others is strengthened.

- We grow when we pray. By uniting our wills with God's we can see ourselves making progress toward becoming more like him. Our faith is flexed.

- We see God answer. Friends are healed. Children begin a relationship with Jesus. Patience appears in the face of trials. Jobs are provided. Our spirits expand.

There is no other exercise that yields more results in our souls than prayer. Want to get your soul in shape? How about bending those knees?

Imitate those who through faith and patience inherit what has been promised.
HEBREWS 6:12

Since we are surrounded by such a great cloud of witnesses, let us throw off everything that hinders and the sin that so easily entangles, and let us run with perseverance the race marked out for us. Let us fix our eyes on Jesus, the author and perfecter of our faith, who for the joy set before him endured the cross, scorning its shame, and sat down at the right hand of the throne of God.
HEBREWS 12:1–2

Make my joy complete by being like-minded, having the same love, being one in spirit and purpose. Do nothing out of selfish ambition or vain conceit, but in humility consider others better than yourselves. Each of you should look not only to your own interests, but also to the interests of others. Your attitude should be the same as that of Christ Jesus.
PHILIPPIANS 2:2–5

Whatever happens, conduct yourselves in a manner worthy of the gospel of Christ. ... Stand firm in one spirit, contending as one ... for the faith of the gospel.
PHILIPPIANS 1:27

Jesus said, "This, then, is how you should pray: "'Our Father in heaven, hallowed be your name, your kingdom come, your will be done on earth as it is in heaven.""

MATTHEW 6:9–10

Whatever was to my profit I now consider loss for the sake of Christ. What is more, I consider everything a loss compared to the surpassing greatness of knowing Christ Jesus my Lord, for whose sake I have lost all things. I consider them rubbish, that I may gain Christ.

PHILIPPIANS 3:7–8

Jesus said, "Do not worry, saying, 'What shall we eat?' or 'What shall we drink?' or 'What shall we wear?'… Seek first God's kingdom and his righteousness, and all these things will be given to you as well."

MATTHEW 6:31, 33

Jesus said, "I tell you, use worldly wealth to gain friends for yourselves, so that when it is gone, you will be welcomed into eternal dwellings."

LUKE 16:9

Blessed is the man
　　who does not walk in the counsel of the wicked
or stand in the way of sinners
　　or sit in the seat of mockers.
But his delight is in the law of the LORD,
　　and on his law he meditates day and night.

PSALM 1:1–2

Someone will say, "You have faith; I have deeds." Show me your faith without deeds, and I will show you my faith by what I do.

JAMES 2:18

We fix our eyes not on what is seen, but on what is unseen. For what is seen is temporary, but what is unseen is eternal.

2 CORINTHIANS 4:18

Whatever you do, work at it with all your heart, as working for the Lord, not for men, since you know that you will receive an inheritance from the Lord as a reward. It is the Lord Christ you are serving.

COLOSSIANS 3:23–24

DEVOTIONAL THOUGHT
ON PRIORITIES

We're surrounded by options! Do we serve in the nursery or sing in the choir? Should we send our children to a public school or a Christian school, or should we teach them at home? How do we choose among the myriad ways to spend a day? A week? A lifetime?

We prioritize. *Priority* is defined as "that which is superior in rank or position," as something meriting prior attention. For Christians, God deserves our prior attention as do his Word, his people and his work.

A careful study of Scripture helps us set priorities. It underlines the value of spending time with God. It spells out the responsibilities of our relationships. It outlines guidance on work and service. We can order our options by taking a biblical look at our lives, designating our primary responsibilities and then devoting our prime time to meeting them.

Woodrow Wilson pledged, "I would rather fail in the cause that will someday triumph than triumph in a cause that will one day fail." What's our triumphant cause? God? Family? Work? Identify it first. Then we can order our options around it.

Jesus said, "In this world you will have trouble. But take heart! I have overcome the world."
JOHN 16:33

Endure hardship ... like a good soldier of Christ Jesus.
2 TIMOTHY 2:3

It has been granted to you on behalf of Christ not only to believe on him, but also to suffer for him.
PHILIPPIANS 1:29

[The Messiah] was despised and rejected by men,
   a man of sorrows, and familiar with suffering.
ISAIAH 53:3

Just as the sufferings of Christ flow over into our lives, so also through Christ our comfort overflows.
2 CORINTHIANS 1:5

Our present sufferings are not worth comparing with the glory that will be revealed in us.
ROMANS 8:18

God knows the way that I take;
   when he has tested me,
   I will come forth as gold.
JOB 23:10

The LORD disciplines those he loves.

PROVERBS 3:12

If you are insulted because of the name of Christ, you are blessed, for the Spirit of glory and of God rests on you.

1 PETER 4:14

We also rejoice in our sufferings, because we know that suffering produces perseverance; perseverance, character; and character, hope.

ROMANS 5:3–4

Consider it pure joy ... whenever you face trials of many kinds, because you know that the testing of your faith develops perseverance.

JAMES 1:2–3

God has not despised or disdained
the suffering of the afflicted one;
he has not hidden his face from him
but has listened to his cry for help.

PSALM 22:24

For Christ's sake, I delight in weaknesses, in insults, in hardships, in persecutions, in difficulties. For when I

am weak, then I am strong.
2 CORINTHIANS 12:10

A righteous man may have many troubles,
> but the LORD delivers him from them all.

PSALM 34:19

*Blessed is the man who perseveres under trial, because
when he has stood the test, he will receive the crown of
life that God has promised to those who love him.*
JAMES 1:12

*Because Christ himself suffered when he was tempted,
he is able to help those who are being tempted.*
HEBREWS 2:18

When I called, you answered me; LORD,
> you made me bold and stouthearted.

PSALM 138:3

*The Spirit helps us in our weakness. We do not know
what we ought to pray for, but the Spirit himself inter-
cedes for us with groans that words cannot express.*
ROMANS 8:26

PROBLEMS

Our struggle is not against flesh and blood, but against the rulers, against the authorities, against the powers of this dark world and against the spiritual forces of evil in the heavenly realms.

EPHESIANS 6:12

Fight the good fight of the faith. Take hold of the eternal life to which you were called.

1 TIMOTHY 6:12

Let the beloved of the LORD rest secure in him,
    for he shields him all day long,
    and the one the LORD loves
    rests between his shoulders.

DEUTERONOMY 33:12

In the day of trouble
    the LORD will keep me safe in his dwelling;
he will hide me in the shelter of his tabernacle
    and set me high upon a rock.

PSALM 27:5

You have been my refuge, O God,
    a strong tower against the foe.
I long to dwell in your tent forever
    and take refuge in the shelter of your wings.

PSALM 61:3–4

P R O B L E M S

He who dwells in the shelter of the Most High
　　will rest in the shadow of the Almighty.

PSALM 91:1

You have been a refuge for the poor, O LORD,
　　a refuge for the needy in his distress,
a shelter from the storm
　　and a shade from the heat.

ISAIAH 25:4

We wait in hope for the LORD;
　　he is our help and our shield.

PSALM 33:20

DEVOTIONAL THOUGHT
ON PROBLEMS

Unemployment. Divorce. Infertility. The death of a father. The illness of a child. The cruelty of an acquaintance.

There comes a time when our faith is tested deliberately by God—not so we will be overcome—but that we might grasp the validity of our faith and know it to be real. From God's hand comes the cumulative exam designed to reinforce our learning about him and his work in our lives.

Someone likened this process to the kite flyer who takes the string of a kite and runs until the kite ascends into the sky. The kite will not rise without the wind. Wind is necessary to flying a kite, and kites rise not *with* the wind, but *against* it. So it is with us. We will not rise to patience and maturity unless we ascend against trials.

We must meet our test not with the bleary eyes of a worried novice but with the confidence of a student who is well-acquainted with the words of the Professor. Layer upon layer, God is educating us about how he has worked in our lives and in the lives of those we love.

God said, "Let us make man in our image, in our likeness, and let them rule over the fish of the sea and the birds of the air, over the livestock, over all the earth, and over all the creatures that move along the ground." So God created man in his own image, in the image of God he created him; male and female he created them.

GENESIS 1:26–27

"Before I formed you in the womb I knew you, before you were born I set you apart," says the LORD.

JEREMIAH 1:5

From one man God made every nation of men, that they should inhabit the whole earth; and God determined the times set for them and the exact places where they should live ... "For in God we live and move and have our being."

ACTS 17:26, 28

Do you not know that your body is a temple of the Holy Spirit, who is in you, whom you have received from God? You are not your own; you were bought at a price. Therefore honor God with your body.

1 CORINTHIANS 6:19–20

GOD'S WORDS OF LIFE ON

SELF-IMAGE

Jesus said, "Are not two sparrows sold for a penny? Yet not one of them will fall to the ground apart from the will of your Father. And even the very hairs of your head are all numbered. So don't be afraid; you are worth more than many sparrows."

MATTHEW 10:29–31

We are God's workmanship, created in Christ Jesus to do good works, which God prepared in advance for us to do.

EPHESIANS 2:10

You have put on the new self, which is being renewed in knowledge in the image of its Creator.

COLOSSIANS 3:10

God chose to give us birth through the word of truth, that we might be a kind of firstfruits of all he created.

JAMES 1:18

For God chose us in him before the creation of the world to be holy and blameless in his sight. In love he predestined us to be adopted as his sons through Jesus Christ, in accordance with his pleasure and will—to the praise of his glorious grace, which he has freely given us in the One he loves.

EPHESIANS 1:4–6

This is what the LORD says—he who created you, O Jacob, he who formed you, O Israel: "Fear not, for I have redeemed you; I have summoned you by name; you are mine."

ISAIAH 43:1

The LORD your God is with you,
    he is mighty to save.
He will take great delight in you,
    he will quiet you with his love,
    he will rejoice over you with singing.

ZEPHANIAH 3:17

DEVOTIONAL THOUGHT
ON SELF-IMAGE

There is only one true mirror of who we are. Only one source can accurately reflect our image back to us. If you want to know who you are, you must look to the One who knows you better than all others.

What can you discover?

- God made you in a marvelous way! "You created my inmost being; you knit me together in my mother's womb. I praise you because I am fearfully and wonderfully made" (Psalm 139:13–14). From your toes to your nose, you are the handiwork of God.

- God loved you enough to die for you even when you didn't deserve it. "While we were still sinners, Christ died for us" (Romans 5:8). Yes, you see the sin. But God covers it all with forgiveness.

- God makes you new and clean, no matter what might have happened in the past. "If anyone is in Christ, he is a new creation; the old has gone, the new has come!" (2 Corinthians 5:17). God dresses us in a brand new outfit—one of hope.

When you're wondering just who you are, don't look to the people around you. The only true reflection of your identity comes from God himself.

SPIRITUAL GROWTH

Jesus said, "Remain in me, and I will remain in you. No branch can bear fruit by itself; it must remain in the vine. Neither can you bear fruit unless you remain in me. I am the vine; you are the branches. If a man remains in me and I in him, he will bear much fruit; apart from me you can do nothing ... If you remain in me and my words remain in you, ask whatever you wish, and it will be given you. This is to my Father's glory, that you bear much fruit, showing yourselves to be my disciples."

JOHN 15:4–5, 7–8

Jesus said, "Whoever lives by the truth comes into the light, so that it may be seen plainly that what he has done has been done through God."

JOHN 3:21

"For you who revere my name, the sun of righteousness will rise with healing in its wings," says the LORD.

MALACHI 4:2

It is the LORD your God you must follow, and him you must revere. Keep his commands and obey him; serve him and hold fast to him.

DEUTERONOMY 13:4

SPIRITUAL GROWTH

The one who sows to please the Spirit, from the Spirit will reap eternal life.
GALATIANS 6:8

Forgetting what is behind and straining toward what is ahead, I press on toward the goal to win the prize for which God has called me heavenward in Christ Jesus.
PHILIPPIANS 3:13–14

Jesus said, "Whoever believes in me, as the Scripture has said, streams of living water will flow from within him."
JOHN 7:38

Do your best to present yourself to God as one approved, a workman who does not need to be ashamed and who correctly handles the word of truth.
2 TIMOTHY 2:15

Jesus said, "Whoever finds his life will lose it, and whoever loses his life for my sake will find it."
MATTHEW 10:39

Like newborn babies, crave pure spiritual milk, so that by it you may grow up in your salvation, now that you have tasted that the Lord is good.
1 PETER 2:2–3

SPIRITUAL GROWTH

The fruit of the Spirit is love, joy, peace, patience, kindness, goodness, faithfulness, gentleness and self-control. Against such things there is no law. Those who belong to Christ Jesus have crucified the sinful nature with its passions and desires. Since we live by the Spirit, let us keep in step with the Spirit.

GALATIANS 5:22–25

We will no longer be infants, tossed back and forth by the waves, and blown here and there by every wind of teaching and by the cunning and craftiness of men in their deceitful scheming. Instead, speaking the truth in love, we will in all things grow up into him who is the Head, that is, Christ.

EPHESIANS 4:14–15

Those who live in accordance with the Spirit have their minds set on what the Spirit desires.

ROMANS 8:5

Grow in the grace and knowledge of our Lord and Savior Jesus Christ. To him be glory both now and forever!

2 PETER 3:18

DEVOTIONAL THOUGHT ON SPIRITUAL GROWTH

Love, joy, peace, patience, kindness, goodness, faithfulness, gentleness and self-control. This is the Bible's official "fruit of the Spirit." We know about fruit that grows on a vine. But what is spiritual fruit?

The fruit is the result of God's purity and perfection. It's God's nature exhibited in us. When we start to grow God's characteristics, we don't lose our own personalities. The fruit of the Spirit is God's characteristics exhibited in our *own* unique personalities. God's nature is exhibited through the person he has made us to be.

We can grow God's fruit in our lives by:

- Picking a fruit we'd like to see God develop. Pray for him to grow it in our lives.

- Studying one fruit at a time. What we think of as patience may not be what Paul meant.

- Journaling the growth of this fruit in our lives. We can write about opportunities for it to be revealed and celebrate when we see these fruits by keeping a record of them.

Exhibiting the fruit of the Spirit is living life like God—being the fruity kind of folks he made us to be!

STRESS

In the day of my trouble I will call to you, O LORD,
    for you will answer me.

PSALM 86:7

In my distress I called to the LORD;
    I called out to my God.
From his temple he heard my voice;
    my cry came to his ears.

2 SAMUEL 22:7

Cast your cares on the LORD
    and he will sustain you;
        he will never let the righteous fall.

PSALM 55:22

Praise be to the Lord, to God our Savior,
    who daily bears our burdens.

PSALM 68:19

When you pass through the waters,
    I will be with you;
and when you pass through the rivers,
    they will not sweep over you.
When you walk through the fire,
    you will not be burned;
        the flames will not set you ablaze.

For I am the LORD, your God.

ISAIAH 43:2–3

Submit to God and be at peace with him;
in this way prosperity will come to you. ...
What you decide on will be done,
     and light will shine on your ways.

JOB 22:21, 28

LORD, you establish peace for us;
     all that we have accomplished
     you have done for us.

ISAIAH 26:12

You will keep in perfect peace
     him whose mind is steadfast,
     because he trusts in you.
Trust in the LORD forever,
     for the LORD, the LORD, is the Rock eternal.

ISAIAH 26:3–4

*May the Lord of peace himself give you peace at all
times and in every way. The Lord be with all of you.*

2 THESSALONIANS 3:16

When God gives any man wealth and possessions, and enables him to enjoy them, to accept his lot and be happy in his work—this is a gift of God. He seldom reflects on the days of his life, because God keeps him occupied with gladness of heart.

ECCLESIASTES 5:19–20

I will listen to what God the LORD will say;
    he promises peace to his people.

PSALM 85:8

Since we have been justified through faith, we have peace with God through our Lord Jesus Christ, through whom we have gained access by faith into this grace in which we now stand. And we rejoice in the hope of the glory of God.

ROMANS 5:1–2

Jesus said, "Come to me, all you who are weary and burdened, and I will give you rest. Take my yoke upon you and learn from me, for I am gentle and humble in heart, and you will find rest for your souls. For my yoke is easy and my burden is light."

MATTHEW 11:28–30

This is what the Sovereign LORD, the Holy One of Israel, says: "In repentance and rest is your salvation, in quietness and trust is your strength."

ISAIAH 30:15

The people in Judah said, "The strength of the laborers is giving out, and there is so much rubble that we cannot rebuild the wall." ... After I looked things over, I stood up and said ... "Remember the Lord, who is great and awesome."

NEHEMIAH 4:10, 14

Because so many people were coming and going that the disciples did not even have a chance to eat, Jesus said to them, "Come with me by yourselves to a quiet place and get some rest."

MARK 6:31

"I will refresh the weary and satisfy the faint," says the LORD Almighty.

JEREMIAH 31:25

By the seventh day God had finished the work he had been doing; so on the seventh day he rested from all his work.

GENESIS 2:2

173

There remains, then, a Sabbath-rest for the people of God; for anyone who enters God's rest also rests from his own work, just as God did from his. Let us, therefore, make every effort to enter that rest.

HEBREWS 4:9–11

The LORD makes me lie down in green pastures,
he leads me beside quiet waters,
    he restores my soul.
He guides me in paths of righteousness
    for his name's sake.

PSALM 23:2–3

DEVOTIONAL THOUGHT
ON STRESS

It's reported that Americans consume about three tons of aspirin a day. That adds up to quite a lot of stress and pain!

Current studies dispute the claim that stress results only from crisis events such as death, divorce, illness and unemployment. Now stress is also linked with a succession of small struggles, heaped one upon another. Whether the cause is life-threatening or simply inconvenient, stress is a human reaction to the real limits of life. It's the predicament of trying to respond to limitless demands with limited resources.

But there is a prescription for stress. Jesus beckons, "Come to me, all you who are weary and burdened, and I will give you rest." We can ask him to shoulder our load, to share the yoke of stress with us. Even three tons of aspirin a day won't get rid of all our stress, but carrying the load with Jesus is a lot easier than carrying it all alone.

Heavy-laden living can weigh us down—or it can lead us to the limitless resources of God, whose "yoke is easy" and whose "burden is light."

We have different gifts, according to the grace given us. If a man's gift is prophesying, let him use it in proportion to his faith. If it is serving, let him serve; if it is teaching, let him teach; if it is encouraging, let him encourage; if it is contributing to the needs of others, let him give generously; if it is leadership, let him govern diligently; if it is showing mercy, let him do it cheerfully.
ROMANS 12:6–8

God's gifts and his call are irrevocable.
ROMANS 11:29

The LORD gives strength to his people.
PSALM 29:11

The LORD bestows favor and honor;
no good thing does he withhold
　　from those whose walk is blameless.
PSALM 84:11

To the [one] who pleases him, God gives wisdom, knowledge and happiness.
ECCLESIASTES 2:26

　[Jesus told this parable:] "A man going on a journey ... called his servants and entrusted his property to them.

TALENTS

To one he gave five talents of money, to another two talents, and to another one talent, each according to his ability. Then he went on his journey. The man who had received the five talents went at once and put his money to work and gained five more. So also, the one with the two talents gained two more. But the man who had received the one talent went off, dug a hole in the ground and hid his master's money.

After a long time the master of those servants returned and settled accounts with them. The man who had received the five talents brought the other five. 'Master,' he said, 'you entrusted me with five talents. See, I have gained five more.' His master replied, 'Well done, good and faithful servant! You have been faithful with a few things; I will put you in charge of many things. Come and share your master's happiness!'

The man with the two talents also came. 'Master,' he said, 'you entrusted me with two talents; see, I have gained two more.' His master replied, 'Well done, good and faithful servant! You have been faithful with a few things; I will put you in charge of many things. Come and share your master's happiness!'

Then the man who had received the one talent came. 'Master,' he said, 'I knew that you are a hard man, harvesting where you have not sown and gathering where you have not scattered seed. So I was afraid and went out and hid your talent in the ground. See, here is what belongs to you.' His master replied, 'You wicked, lazy servant! So you knew that I harvest where I have not sown and gather where I have not scattered seed? Well then, you should have put my money on deposit with the bankers, so that when I returned I would have received it back with interest. Take the talent from him and give it to the one who has the ten talents. For everyone who has will be given more, and he will have an abundance.'"

MATTHEW 25:14–29

In Christ Jesus you have been enriched in every way— in all your speaking and in all your knowledge.

1 CORINTHIANS 1:5

Each man has his own gift from God; one has this gift, another has that.

1 CORINTHIANS 7:7

DEVOTIONAL THOUGHT
ON TALENTS

Think about the talents and skills you've discovered so far in your life. As you create a mental list, consider all spheres of your life: hobbies, work, sports, family activities. God has uniquely created you with certain aptitudes and has allowed you many experiences designed to develop them. Be sure to include your growing up years and school activities as well as your adult years.

Now, get out a sheet of paper and actually *write down* what you're good at. Perhaps you'll want to tuck the sheet of paper in your Bible. Pull it out when you need encouragement or a reminder of your abilities.

Before you put your list away, go back through it and asterisk the items that currently hold the greatest interest for you. To the side of the asterisked items, jot down ways in which you could contribute this skill or ability. Finally, pray and ask God where and when he would have you invest this ability for his purposes.

Thanks be to God, who always leads us in triumphal procession in Christ and through us spreads everywhere the fragrance of the knowledge of him.

2 CORINTHIANS 2:14

By prayer and petition, with thanksgiving, present your requests to God.

PHILIPPIANS 4:6

Give thanks in all circumstances, for this is God's will for you in Christ Jesus.

1 THESSALONIANS 5:18

Thanks be to God! He gives us the victory through our Lord Jesus Christ.

1 CORINTHIANS 15:57

I will give thanks to the LORD
    because of his righteousness
    and will sing praise to the name of the LORD
        Most High.

PSALM 7:17

Give thanks to the LORD, for he is good;
    his love endures forever.
Let the redeemed of the LORD say this.

PSALM 107:1–2

THANKFULNESS

Just as you received Christ Jesus as Lord, continue to live in him, rooted and built up in him, strengthened in the faith as you were taught, and overflowing with thankfulness.

COLOSSIANS 2:6–7

Give thanks to the LORD for his unfailing love
    and his wonderful deeds for men.

PSALM 107:21

You turned my wailing into dancing;
    you removed my sackcloth
    and clothed me with joy,
that my heart may sing to you and not be silent.
    O LORD my God, I will give you thanks forever.

PSALM 30:11–12

Come, let us sing for joy to the LORD;
    let us shout aloud to the Rock of our salvation.
Let us come before him with thanksgiving
    and extol him with music and song.

PSALM 95:1–2

Thanks be to God for his indescribable gift!
2 CORINTHIANS 9:15

Give thanks to the LORD, call on his name;
    make known among the nations
    what he has done.

1 CHRONICLES 16:8

Praise the LORD.
I will extol the LORD with all my heart
    in the council of the upright
    and in the assembly.
Great are the works of the LORD;
    they are pondered by all who delight in them.

PSALM 111:1–2

Enter his gates with thanksgiving
    and his courts with praise;
give thanks to the LORD
    and praise his name.

PSALM 100:4

I will sacrifice a thank offering to you, O God,
    and call on the name of the LORD.

PSALM 116:17

*Everything God created is good, and nothing is to be
rejected if it is received with thanksgiving.*

1 TIMOTHY 4:4

Arteriosclerosis is a condition in which the arteries that carry blood to the major organs of the body grow tough and refuse to let blood pass. The old-fashioned name for this disease is hardening of the arteries. Hardening of the heart is a spiritual condition in which the heart toughens up and refuses to allow God's power, spirit and love to flow through us. Like arteriosclerosis, this hard-hearted condition can be life-threatening.

The best remedy for this condition, whether well-progressed or in its beginning stages, is thankfulness. Because discontent and ingratitude harden a heart, it stands to reason that praise, gratitude and trust will soften one.

How can we be thankful when we're surrounded by crisis? How can we be grateful when life is turning upside down before our eyes?

We can focus our hearts on this: God's character is utterly and completely consistent. We can thank him always for his constancy and for the fact that he is in control of all that we aren't.

TRUST

Those who know your name will trust in you,
    for you, LORD, have never forsaken
    those who seek you.

PSALM 9:10

Those who trust in the LORD are like Mount Zion,
    which cannot be shaken but endures forever.

PSALM 125:1

It is better to take refuge in the LORD
    than to trust in man.
It is better to take refuge in the LORD
    than to trust in princes.

PSALM 118:8–9

Why are you downcast, O my soul?
    Why so disturbed within me?
Put your hope in God,
    for I will yet praise him,
    my Savior and my God.

PSALM 42:5–6

Whoever gives heed to instruction prospers,
    and blessed is he who trusts in the LORD.

PROVERBS 16:20

TRUST

Blessed is the man who trusts in the LORD,
　　whose confidence is in him.
He will be like a tree planted by the water
　　that sends out its roots by the stream.
It does not fear when heat comes;
　　its leaves are always green.
It has no worries in a year of drought
　　and never fails to bear fruit.

JEREMIAH 17:7–8

Trust in the LORD and do good;
　　dwell in the land and enjoy safe pasture.

PSALM 37:3

Nebuchadnezzar said, "Praise be to the God of
Shadrach, Meshach and Abednego, who has sent his
angel and rescued his servants! They trusted in him and
defied the king's command and were willing to give up
their lives rather than serve or worship any god except
their own God."

DANIEL 3:28

He who trusts in the LORD will prosper.

PROVERBS 28:25

TRUST

Anyone who trusts in Christ will never be put to shame.
ROMANS 10:11

Fear of man will prove to be a snare,
    but whoever trusts in the LORD is kept safe.
PROVERBS 29:25

Trust in the LORD with all your heart
    and lean not on your own understanding.
PROVERBS 3:5

Be strong and take heart,
    all you who hope in the LORD.
PSALM 31:24

The LORD is good,
    a refuge in times of trouble.
He cares for those who trust in him.
NAHUM 1:7

Prick up your ears. God is speaking to you.

What might God be saying to us when our car breaks down on the freeway? When our two-year-old gets his sixth ear infection in as many months? When our pre-teen challenges our authority? When we find out we need a $250 crown on a molar? *Trust me ...*

What might God want us to learn when our husband forgets our anniversary, our best friend breaks the lunch date we scheduled two weeks ago and our ten-year-old borrows our best blanket for a fort and forgets it in the rain? *You are important to me. I love you.*

It is so easy for us to overlook the obvious. When we lift our heads from the muddled desert of our circum-stances, we can look up and see—in the middle of our hurt and pain—the God who guides us. *Trust me ...*

Whoever sows sparingly will also reap sparingly, and whoever sows generously will also reap generously. Each man should give what he has decided in his heart to give, not reluctantly or under compulsion, for God loves a cheerful giver. And God is able to make all grace abound to you, so that in all things at all times, having all that you need, you will abound in every good work. As it is written: "He has scattered abroad his gifts to the poor; his righteousness endures forever."

Now he who supplies seed to the sower and bread for food will also supply and increase your store of seed and will enlarge the harvest of your righteousness. You will be made rich in every way so that you can be generous on every occasion, and through us your generosity will result in thanksgiving to God.

2 CORINTHIANS 9:6–11

Jesus said, "'Love the Lord your God with all your heart and with all your soul and with all your mind.' This is the first and greatest commandment. And the second is like it: 'Love your neighbor as yourself.'"

MATTHEW 22:37–39

Who may ascend the hill of the LORD?
Who may stand in his holy place?

He who has clean hands and a pure heart,
    who does not lift up his soul to an idol
    or swear by what is false.
He will receive blessing from the LORD
    and vindication from God his Savior.

PSALM 24:3–5

What does the LORD require of you?
To act justly and to love mercy
    and to walk humbly with your God.

MICAH 6:8

Be careful that you do not forget the LORD your God,
failing to observe his commands, his laws and his
decrees. … Otherwise, when you eat and are satisfied,
when you build fine houses and settle down, and when
your herds and flocks grow large and your silver and
gold increase and all you have is multiplied, then your
heart will become proud and you will forget the LORD
your God.

DEUTERONOMY 8:11–14

Do to others as you would have them do to you.

LUKE 6:31

Speak and act as those who are going to be judged by the law that gives freedom, because judgment without mercy will be shown to anyone who has not been merciful. Mercy triumphs over judgment!

JAMES 2:12–13

A wife of noble character who can find?
     She is worth far more than rubies. ...
She opens her arms to the poor
     and extends her hands to the needy. ...
She is clothed with strength and dignity;
     she can laugh at the days to come.
She speaks with wisdom,
     and faithful instruction is on her tongue. ...
Charm is deceptive,
     and beauty is fleeting;
but a woman who fears the LORD
     is to be praised.

PROVERBS 31:10, 20, 25–26, 30

Whatever is true, whatever is noble, whatever is right, whatever is pure, whatever is lovely, whatever is admirable—if anything is excellent or praiseworthy— think about such things.

PHILIPPIANS 4:8

DEVOTIONAL THOUGHT
ON VALUES

The measure of a woman's character can be found in what she would do if she knew she would never be found out. The woman of integrity demonstrates a character that is as pure beneath the surface as it is above. She is authentic. Her values are woven into a moral code that permeates her whole life.

The Bible relates many examples of women of integrity: Jochebed had the vision to resist an oppressive society and save her son Moses. Deborah's faith led her to courageously serve God in an amoral culture. Abigail dared to venture out to aid God's chosen leader, David. Esther courageously risked her own life to save her people. Ruth faithfully supported her mother-in-law and sustained her family heritage.

If we want to draw someone's attention to the God we love, we will be the same person on the inside as we are on the outside. As William Dyer put it, "Either be what thou seemest, or be what thou art."

WISDOM

If you accept my words
    and store up my commands within you
turning your ear to wisdom
    and applying your heart to understanding,
and if you call out for insight
    and cry aloud for understanding,
and if you look for it as for silver
    and search for it as for hidden treasure,
then you will understand the fear of the LORD
    and find the knowledge of God.
For the LORD gives wisdom,
    and from his mouth come knowledge and
understanding.

PROVERBS 2:1–6

The fear of the Lord—that is wisdom. ...
JOB 28:28

*Jesus said, "Everyone who hears these words of mine
and puts them into practice is like a wise man who
built his house on the rock. The rain came down, the
streams rose, and the winds blew and beat against
that house; yet it did not fall, because it had its foundation on the rock.*

MATTHEW 7:24–25

WISDOM

Get wisdom, get understanding. ...
Do not forsake wisdom, and she will protect you;
> love her, and she will watch over you.
Wisdom is supreme; therefore get wisdom.
> Though it cost all you have, get understanding.

PROVERBS 4:5–7

"I guide you in the way of wisdom
> and lead you along straight paths.
When you walk, your steps will not be hampered;
> when you run, you will not stumble," says the
LORD.

PROVERBS 4:11–12

Trust in the LORD with all your heart
> and lean not on your own understanding;
in all your ways acknowledge him,
> and he will make your paths straight.

PROVERBS 3:5–6

Do you not know?
> Have you not heard?
The LORD is the everlasting God,
> the Creator of the ends of the earth.

He will not grow tired or weary,
 and his understanding no one can fathom.

ISAIAH 40:28

Whether you turn to the right or to the left, your ears will hear a voice behind you, saying, "This is the way; walk in it."

ISAIAH 30:21

The wisdom that comes from heaven is first of all pure; then peace-loving, considerate, submissive, full of mercy and good fruit, impartial and sincere.

JAMES 3:17

What makes a wise guy wise?

In part, it's being smart. The Hebrew word for wisdom, *hokmah*, implies knowledge. A person with superior mental ability in a given category is considered "wise."

But that's not all. *Hokmah* is most accurately translated as a "skill for living." Those who embroidered lavish robes for the priests of the Old Testament were considered by God to be wise. They had the knowledge and the expertise to put know-how into action.

You won't be wise just by being smart. Wisdom is knowing what to do with what you know. It's a skill for living life. And those who are interested in becoming wise guys will study life and then apply what they learn in the way they live.

Dear Lord, please make me wise. Give me both the knowledge and the ability to know what to do with this knowledge. Make me one who is truly skilled for living, not because I can quote a list of biblical values, but because I know how to apply those values and truths to the way I live.

Amen.

WORRY

Do not be anxious about anything, but in everything, by prayer and petition, with thanksgiving, present your requests to God. And the peace of God, which transcends all understanding, will guard your hearts and your minds in Christ Jesus.

PHILIPPIANS 4:6–7

Do not be afraid, little flock, for your Father has been pleased to give you the kingdom.

LUKE 12:32

The LORD himself goes before you and will be with you; he will never leave you nor forsake you. Do not be afraid; do not be discouraged.

DEUTERONOMY 31:8

Be still, and know that I am God;
    I will be exalted among the nations,
    I will be exalted in the earth.
The LORD Almighty is with us;
    the God of Jacob is our fortress.

PSALM 46:10-11

The LORD blesses his people with peace.

PSALM 29:11

Jesus said, "Do not worry about your life, what you will eat or drink; or about your body, what you will wear. Is not life more important than food, and the body more important than clothes? Look at the birds of the air; they do not sow or reap or store away in barns, and yet your heavenly Father feeds them. Are you not much more valuable than they? Who of you by worrying can add a single hour to his life?

"And why do you worry about clothes? See how the lilies of the field grow. They do not labor or spin. Yet I tell you that not even Solomon in all his splendor was dressed like one of these. If that is how God clothes the grass of the field, which is here today and tomorrow is thrown into the fire, will he not much more clothe you, O you of little faith? So do not worry, saying, 'What shall we eat?' or 'What shall we drink?' or 'What shall we wear?' For the pagans run after all these things, and your heavenly Father knows that you need them. But seek first his kingdom and his righteousness, and all these things will be given to you as well. Therefore do not worry about tomorrow, for tomorrow will worry about itself."

MATTHEW 6:25-34

WORRY

Those who trust in the LORD are like Mount Zion,
which cannot be shaken but endures forever.

PSALM 125:1

Cast your cares on the LORD
and he will sustain you;
he will never let the righteous fall.

PSALM 55:22

Do not fear, for I am with you;
do not be dismayed, for I am your God.
I will strengthen you and help you;
I will uphold you with my righteous right hand.

ISAIAH 41:10

Cast all your anxiety on God because he cares for you.
1 PETER 5:7

When I am afraid,
I will trust in you.
In God, whose word I praise,
in God I trust; I will not be afraid.
What can mortal man do to me?

PSALM 56:3–4

Moses stands on the edge of the Red Sea with the Israelites bleating like scared sheep while the Egyptians bear down upon them. "It would have been better to serve the Egyptians than to die in the desert!" baaa-aaahed (Exodus 14:12).

Moses' response to the Israelites is much ~~...~~ ~~...~~ves ~~...~~ns of ~~...~~irm ~~...~~ bring ~~...~~, you need only to be still" (Exodus 14:13–14).

Who are the Egyptians bearing down on us today? Bills to be paid? Unkind critics? And what is the Red Sea that threatens to hem us in from hope? Unemployment? Illness? Confusion about our personal value?

Where the tendency may be to worry, panic and run, God tells us that we "need only to be still." This day, this minute, stuck between the Egyptians and the Red Sea, we can choose to lay aside panic and instead be still.

WORSHIP

Great is the LORD and most worthy of praise;
>   his greatness no one can fathom.

PSALM 145:3

Holy, holy, holy is the LORD Almighty;
>   the whole earth is full of his glory.

ISAIAH 6:3

*You are worthy, our Lord and God, to receive glory and
honor and power, for you created all things, and by
your will they were created and have their being.*

REVELATION 4:11

Come, let us bow down in worship,
>   let us kneel before the LORD our Maker;
for he is our God
>   and we are the people of his pasture,
>   the flock under his care.

PSALM 95:6–7

*Since we are receiving a kingdom that cannot be
shaken, let us be thankful, and so worship God accept-
ably with reverence and awe.*

HEBREWS 12:28

The LORD is my strength and my song;
> he has become my salvation.
He is my God, and I will praise him,
> my father's God, and I will exalt him.

EXODUS 15:2

Jesus said, "A time is coming and has now come when the true worshipers will worship the Father in spirit and truth, for they are the kind of worshipers the Father seeks. God is spirit, and his worshipers must worship in spirit and in truth."

JOHN 4:23–24

I will praise you, O LORD, with all my heart;
> I will tell of all your wonders.
I will be glad and rejoice in you;
> I will sing praise to your name, O Most High.

PSALM 9:1–2

Praise be to the God and Father of our Lord Jesus Christ, who has blessed us in the heavenly realms with every spiritual blessing in Christ.

EPHESIANS 1:3

I will praise you forever
    for what you have done, O LORD;
    in your name I will hope,
    for your name is good.
    I will praise you in the presence of your saints.
PSALM 52:9

The LORD lives! Praise be to my Rock!
    Exalted be God, the Rock, my Savior!
2 SAMUEL 22:47

Praise the LORD, O my soul,
    and forget not all his benefits—
who forgives all your sins
    and heals all your diseases,
who redeems your life from the pit
    and crowns you with love and compassion.
PSALM 103:2–4

Let us continually offer to God a sacrifice of praise—the
~~~~~ ~fess his name.

~~~~~~~~~~~~~~~~~~~~~~~~~ life, LORD,
    my lips will ~
I will praise you as long as ~

DEVOTIONAL THOUGHT ON WORSHIP

We mouth hymns while staring at the dandruff on the suit jacket of the man in front of us. We pass the collection plate while wondering if we have enough money left to pay the phone bill, the heating bill, the charge cards. We prop our Bibles open but close our minds to the message from the pulpit and instead ponder a problem with our child. We go through the motions of worship with our heads but keep our hearts out of the process.

In order to truly worship God we must use more than our heads. We must employ our hearts.

How does it *feel* to consider God's power in creation? What happens to our outlook on life when a hymn describes God's provision for the most daily of our needs? What does God want us to *do* in response to what we've heard?

It's not enough to recognize God with our heads. We must respond to him with our hearts. Worship is both recognizing and responding to God. It's the plunging of both head and heart into the wonders of his Person and experiencing and expressing the truth of what we find there.

MOTHERS OF

M⌄PS.

PRESCHOOLERS

MOPS stands for Mothers of Preschoolers, a program designed for mothers with children under school age. Approximately 2,500 MOPS groups meet in churches throughout the United States, Canada, and 11 other countries to meet the needs of more than 100,000 women each year. The women are of many ages and backgrounds, but share the same desire—to be the best mothers they can be. To receive information such as how to join a MOPS group, or how to receive other MOPS resources such as *MOM-Sense* newsletter, call or write:

MOPS International,
P.O. Box 102200,
Denver, CO 80250-2200
Phone 1-800-929-1287
E-mail: Info@MOPS.org
Web site: http://www.MOPS.org

To learn how to start a MOPS group, call 1-888-910-MOPS. For MOPS products call The MOPShop at 1-888-545-4040.